do yourself a favor... forgive

LEARN HOW TO TAKE CONTROL OF YOUR LIFE THROUGH FORGIVENESS

JOYCE MEYER

LARGE PRINT

Unless otherwise indicated, Scriptures are taken from the Amplified® Bible. Copyright © 1954, 1962, 1965, 1987 by The Lockman Foundation. Used by permission.

Scriptures noted NKJV are taken from the NEW KING JAMES VERSION. Copyright © 1979, 1980, 1982, Thomas Nelson, Inc., Publishers.

FaithWords
Hachette Book Group
237 Park Avenue
New York, NY 10017
www.faithwords.com

Printed in the United States of America

RRD-IN

First Edition: April 2012
10 9 8 7 6 5 4 3 2 1

FaithWords is a division of Hachette Book Group, Inc.

The FaithWords name and logo are trademarks of Hachette Book Group, Inc.

The Hachette Speakers Bureau provides a wide range of authors for speaking events. To find out more, go to www.hachettespeakersbu reau.com or call (866) 376-6591.

The publisher is not responsible for websites (or their content) that are not owned by the publisher.

Library of Congress Control Number: 2011939590
ISBN: 9781455513383

CONTENTS

INTRODUCTION

Jesus came that our sins might be forgiven and we would be restored to an intimate relationship with God through Him. His free gift of forgiveness is beautiful and beyond comparison. What God gives us freely He expects us to also give freely to others. Because we have received God's forgiveness we can forgive others who sin against us or harm us in any way.

If we don't forgive we will be miserable and our soul will be poisoned with the malignancy of bitterness. I have learned that when I forgive someone who has hurt me, I am actually doing myself a favor, and that knowledge makes it much easier for me to forgive quickly and completely. I would like to be able to say that I learned this principle early in my life and have not wasted precious time in unforgiveness, but I can't. It has taken me decades to learn what I desire to share with you in this book.

Unfortunately, we won't go through life and

never get hurt, wounded, or offended. Experience tells us that life is filled with injustices. However, we can be free from the pain of these wounds by letting them go and trusting God to be our Vindicator and bring justice into our lives.

The roots of unforgiveness are very dangerous. They grow deep below the surface and take hold deep within us. They are insidious because they convince us that because we have been wronged, someone must be punished and that we cannot and will not be happy until they are. We want to be paid back for the pain we have endured, but only God can pay us back, and He will if we trust Him and forgive our enemies as He has told us to do.

I am sure that many who read this book will begin with anger in their hearts. Someone has hurt them or life has disappointed them. My prayer is that their hearts will be opened to God and they will see the urgent importance of living free from any kind of bitterness, resentment, unforgiveness, or offense.

I believe that we have opportunities every week to be offended and become angry, but proper knowledge of God's will gives us the courage to move beyond anger and enjoy the life God has given us. Staying angry at someone who has hurt you is like taking poison hoping that your enemy will die. Our unforgiveness hurts us more than it does anyone else. God never asks us to do anything unless it is going to ultimately be good for us, so we should trust Him and learn to freely forgive.

It is my prayer that as you read this book, you will learn that when you process anger in a healthy manner and when you forgive, the person you're doing a favor for is yourself.

do yourself a
favor...
forgive

CHAPTER
1

It Isn't Fair!

Susanna is a forty-eight-year-old woman who grew up on a remote farm in a tiny Texas town. Her parents were extremely poor, with little income and half a dozen children.

Susanna was the youngest, and her sunny disposition, pretty features, and unusual intelligence served her well from early on. She finished high school and went on to be one of the best salespeople where she worked in a small company that manufactured clothing. Eventually, she started her own business, manufacturing women's apparel. She loved her business; it gave her a sense of accomplishment and value, and she gave herself to it wholeheartedly. She met and married the man of her dreams, and they had two children. As the years progressed, so did her business, and by the time she was in her early forties, she and her husband were running a multimillion-dollar company together.

Susanna and her husband enjoyed all that wealth could provide: a magnificent home, cars, boats, and a summer cottage. Their vacations took them around the world. Their two daughters attended the best schools and enjoyed the most prominent social circles. They grew up and enjoyed successful careers and families of their own. Life could not have been any better, or so they thought. Although the couple attended church occasionally out of a sense of duty, their relationship with God was not personal, nor did they genuinely consider God's will when making decisions. Even the family relationships were more surface ones rather than deep, honest, and intimate.

One day, suddenly and without warning, Susanna learned that her husband was having an affair and that it wasn't the first time. She was shocked and deeply hurt. Not only was he unfaithful, but she also learned he had plunged the company into debt and a tremendous amount of the corporate money was unaccounted for. He had been taking money from the business she started and using it to entertain his girlfriends and live a secret life.

The marriage dissolved quickly, and Susanna was left with a business that was deep in debt and on the verge of collapse. Then the economy tanked and retail sales plunged downward, which resulted in Susanna's company going under. Her anger and bitterness toward her ex-husband, whom she blamed for everything, was increasing daily.

Susanna turned to her children for understanding and comfort, but they resented her for the years she had worked so hard and failed to spend much time with them. They also felt that part of their father's infidelity was due to their mother loving her business more than anything else in the world. They were busy with their own lives and ignored their mother's needs and problems just as they felt she had ignored theirs when they needed her. Susanna needed support, but there was none.

She turned to her sister, but believe it or not she seemed to revel in Susanna's distress. She felt that her years of success and "easy living" had made her selfish and inconsiderate. The rift that ensued between them was massive, and they still don't speak to this day after eight years.

Her children, while polite, don't call often or invite her to visit. Susanna has become increasingly bitter and blames everyone else for her unhappiness. Not once has she considered that some of the problems could have been her fault, and not once has she even considered forgiving and asking for forgiveness.

She is angry with her ex-husband. She is angry with herself for not having seen that her marriage and business were falling apart right before her eyes. She is angry that her children haven't done more for her, and she is angry at God because her life has turned out to be so disappointing.

Who Wouldn't Be Angry?

Most people in this situation would be angry, but they wouldn't have to be if they understood the love of God and knew that He has already provided a way out of this kind of misery. The number of lives that are ruined through anger and unforgiveness is astonishing. Some of them don't know any better, but many of them are Christians who do know better but are unwilling to make the right choice. They live according to their feelings, rather than moving beyond them to do the better thing. They lock themselves in a prison of negative emotions and limp along in life rather than living it fully and vibrantly.

Yes, most people would be angry, but there is a better way: they could do themselves a favor and forgive. They could shake off their disappointment and get reappointed in God. They could look to the future instead of the past. They could learn from their mistakes and endeavor to not make them again.

Although most of us don't find ourselves in such dire circumstances as Susanna was in, there is certainly no end of things to be angry about…the neighbor's dog, the government, taxes, not getting the pay increase that was expected, traffic, a husband who leaves his socks and underwear on the bathroom floor, or the kids showing no appreciation for all you do for them. Then there are the people who say unkind things to us and never apologize, parents who never showed affection, siblings who were favored, false accusations, and on and on the list goes in a never-ending cascade of opportunities to either be angry or forgive and move on.

Our natural reaction is upset, offense, bitterness, anger, and unforgiveness.

But who are we hurting by nursing these negative emotions? The person who committed the offense? Sometimes it does hurt people if we shut them out of our lives through anger, but quite often they don't even know or care that we are angry! We walk around preoccupied with our upset, replaying the offense over and over again in our minds. How much time have you spent imagining what you want to tell the person who made you angry, all the while upsetting yourself more? When we allow ourselves to do this, we actually hurt ourselves much more than the offender.

Medical studies have shown that anger can cause everything from ulcers to a bad attitude. At the very least it is a waste of precious time. Every hour that we stay angry is an hour we have used and will never get back. In Susanna's and her family's case, they wasted years. Think of the times they missed in fellowship because of all the anger among them. Life is unpredictable; we don't know how much time we have left with our loved ones. What a shame it is to deprive ourselves of good memories and relationships because of anger. I also wasted a lot of years being angry and bitter because of injustices done to me early in life. My attitude affected me in many negative ways, and it overflowed onto my family. Angry people always take their anger out on someone because what is in us does come out of us. We may think we have our anger hidden from everyone, but it finds a way to express itself eventually.

The things that happen to us are often not fair, but God will recompense us if we trust and obey Him. Wanting revenge is a normal desire, but it is not one we can indulge in. We want to be paid back for damage done, and God promises to do just that.

For we know Him Who said, Vengeance is
Mine [retribution and the meting out of full
justice rest with Me]; I will repay [I will exact
the compensation], says the Lord. And again,
The Lord will judge and determine and solve
and settle the cause and the cases of His
people.

Hebrews 10:30

This Scripture and others like it have encouraged me to let go of my anger and bitterness and
trust God to repay me in His own way. I strongly
encourage you to take the same leap of faith anytime you feel you have been treated unfairly.

The people we need to forgive usually don't
deserve it and sometimes don't even want it. They
may not know they offended us, or might not care,
yet God asks us to forgive them. It would seem out-
rageously unfair except for the fact that God does
the same things for us that He is asking us to do for
others. He forgives us over and over again and continues loving us unconditionally.

It helps me to forgive if I take the time to remember all the mistakes I have made and needed not
only God's forgiveness, but people's as well. My
husband was very gracious and merciful toward me
during many years while I was working through
a healing process from the trauma of child abuse.

My belief is that "hurting people hurt people." I know that I hurt my family and was unable to build healthy relationships, but I certainly did not do it purposely. It was the result of my own pain and ignorance. I had been hurt, and all I thought about was myself. I was hurting, so I hurt others. I really needed understanding, confrontation at the right time, and loads of forgiveness, and God worked through Dave to give me that. I try to remember now that God often wants to work through me to do the same things for someone else.

Have you ever needed forgiveness—from people as well as from God? I am sure you have. Remember those times, and it will enable you to forgive when you need to.

Please Check Your Anger at the Door

Have you ever watched an old western movie where the cowboys were required to check their weapons at the door before entering a saloon? I have, and it is a good example to use when we think of anger. Anger is like a weapon we carry with us so we can lash out at people who appear to be on the verge of hurting us. Just like the cowboys would pull their pistols to defend themselves unless they checked them at the door, we pull our anger in defense on a regular basis. Let's form a habit of consciously leaving our anger at the door before we enter any-place. Let's refuse to take it with us when we go out for the day. Consciously say, "I am going out today without anger. I am taking love, mercy, and forgiveness with me and will use them generously when needed."

I have found that talking to myself is a big help. I can talk myself into things and out of things. I can talk myself into getting angry and into getting over being angry. Learn to reason with yourself. Say to yourself, "It is a waste of time to stay angry and it is displeasing to God, so I am going to purposely let it go." I remind myself that I am doing myself a favor by choosing peace and refusing anger.

We may not feel like doing the right thing, but we can either live to please God or to please ourselves. If we choose pleasing God, then we will do many things that will be the opposite of what we might feel like doing. We all have feelings, but we are more than our feelings. We also have a free will and can choose what we know will be the best for us.

Anger Is Strong and Destructive

Anger is indignation, vengeance, and wrath. It begins as a feeling and progresses to expression in words and actions if it is not checked. It is one of the strongest passions and is very destructive. God's Word teaches us to control anger because it never produces the righteousness that He desires (James 1:20).

We are instructed by God to be slow to anger. When we feel ourselves starting to boil over with anger, we need to put a lid on it. We can stir ourselves up and make our problems worse by thinking about and talking about them, which equates to feeding them . . . or . . . the minute our feelings start to rise up we can do something about them. Be aggressive against the emotion of anger and say, "I refuse to stay angry. I refuse to take offense. God has given me self-control, and I will use it."

I was told a story about a pastor who invited a guest speaker to his church. The pastor was sitting in the front row of the church listening to the speaker, when without using wisdom the speaker began to say some negative things about the way the pastor handled some of his church business. He was making a general comment and I am sure not intending to offend anyone, but his words were critical and cutting. While the speaker was speaking, the pastor softly repeated in a whisper, "I will not be offended, I will not be offended." He was an older minister who had more wisdom than his speaker. He recognized the zeal of his guest but also knew that the speaker lacked knowledge. The pastor refused to let his guest's words offend him.

I know what this is like because I am on television sharing the Gospel message, and I hear other people in ministry who are not on television make negative statements about "televangelists," which is what they un-lovingly call those of us who are called to the media ministry.

It is very easy to judge someone if we have not walked in their shoes, and when I hear people make unkind comments, I try to remember that they are talking about something they know nothing about. People say things like "Those televangelists are just trying to get people's money." "Those televangelists don't do anything to build the church; they are just out for themselves and are not kingdom-of-God minded." Of course, there are some people in every profession who have impure motives, but to lump everyone into that category is totally wrong and not in agreement with Scripture. When I hear things like this or am told that someone said these things, I decide not to be offended, because it won't change anything and certainly won't do me any good.

When I invite people to receive Jesus Christ on television, our ministry receives an overwhelming response. We send them a book that instructs them to get involved in a good local church, but that might be something that a critic does not know.

I am committed to doing what I know God has called me to do and not to worry about my critics, because I won't answer to them at the end of my life but to God alone.

It is easy to judge others, thinking we know "the whole story." But very few of us do; that's reserved for God. I am sure you have examples of your own, and the best thing to do is to pray for the person whose words brought offense, make a decision not to take the offense, and choose to believe the best of them. We should all pray that we don't hurt others or give offense with our own words.

CHAPTER
2

The Emotion of Anger

People living without God in their lives usually are not disturbed by feeling the emotion of anger—they may even think it is the way to solve problems or the avenue to getting what one wants. Christians are disturbed by anger, though, and even confused by it. As godly individuals, we often think that as Christians, we should not have anger. Then we often feel guilty when we do experience the emotion of anger. We wonder why we get angry when, in fact, that is the last thing we want to do.

I have been a serious student of God's Word for thirty-five years, and I assure you that I have no desire to be angry. I have worked diligently with the Holy Spirit over the years learning how to get over anger and control it. I am a peace lover and desire unity in all my relationships. I despise strife! Yet, recently I suddenly became angrier than I can remember being in a long, long time.

Emotions can flare up quickly. We are not expected not to have them, but we are expected not to let them rule us. God's Word never states that feeling anger is sin. But it does become sinful behavior when we don't manage it properly or when we hang on to it. The apostle Paul instructs that we are not to let the sun set on our anger (Eph. 4:26–27). That indicates that people will experience the emotion of anger, but within a short period of time they should be able to let it go. For me this requires prayer and making a decision that goes beyond how I feel.

Not too long ago I was talking to my aunt on the telephone. Dave and I have provided for her financially for the past several years because she is widowed and her income is not enough to support her properly. I hold her power of attorney, so anytime she has medical needs the health care center where she lives calls me to take care of any medical emergency. I wanted my daughter to be added to the list of people who have authority to make decisions for my aunt so if I were out of town her medical needs would be taken care of. I sent my daughter to my aunt's home with a paper for her to sign, and she became very defensive and refused to sign it. When my daughter relayed this information to me, I immediately without any forethought became so angry that I thought I would burst. I had expected my aunt to merely trust me and do what I asked, so I called her and told her exactly what I thought, reminding her of all I had done for her and that I did not appreciate her selfish behavior. We were both angry and said lots of things that we should not have said.

To be honest, I felt justified in my anger—and that was a mistake. Justifying it allowed me to hold on to it for three days while I waited for her to call me and apologize, and she never did. During those three days I told several people in my family and one friend all about the situation, elaborating on how selfish I thought she was. Of course, that was also a mistake since God's Word teaches us not to do anything to harm another person's reputation, nor to gossip or be a talebearer. Each time I told the story, my anger was given new fuel and it burned hotter than before. I can honestly say that I don't recall having been that angry for that long in years.

What happened? First of all, I was very tired when this situation arose; I realize now that I acted hastily in the way I handled my request. Because I was tired, I didn't take the time to fully explain myself to my aunt, and that opened the door for confusion. Not only was I tired, but I had been dealing with a lot of urgent needs for my aunt and my mom in the few weeks prior to that, and I was feeling pressured and looking for ways to make things easier for me.

On the morning of the fourth day after the incident, I realized that the anger I felt was hindering my intimacy with God and preventing me from being able to properly study God's Word. I kept thinking about the situation and could not get it off my mind, which is usually the case with me until I confront and resolve difficult matters. I started feeling that God wanted me to call her and apologize, and I admit that I really did not want to comply.

The more I opened my heart to God, the more clearly I saw my aunt's side of the situation. She is eighty-four years old and is quickly losing her independence, which is understandably very hard for her. From her point of view, she was probably surprised at the turn of events. Suddenly I had sent papers to her asking her to sign over her health decisions to my daughter if I was out of town, without explaining exactly what that meant. After waiting a few hours because I was dreading making the call, I finally did call and told her I was sorry I had gotten so angry. To my pleasant surprise, she told me she was sorry, too, and that she had acted badly because she was confused. Within two minutes the entire situation was resolved and my peace returned, as did hers.

After the incident I realized I could have and should have handled the situation with a lot more wisdom and concern for her feelings than I had. I genuinely repented before God, not only for staying angry three days, but also for gossiping about the situation to other people.

I wanted to share this story with you simply to show that anger can come quickly, and no matter how "Christian" we are, we are never beyond the temptation to get angry. I am sorry that I let it go for three days, but I am glad I didn't let it become a root of bitterness in my life and continue poisoning my soul for even longer.

God is slow to anger, and we should be the same way. He restrains His wrath—that means self-control. God often turned His anger away and did not stir up wrath (Ps. 78:38). "Turned it away" means He controlled it. Remember, self-control is a Fruit of the Spirit. It is an aspect of God's character that He has shared with us. We see many instances in the Bible when man provoked God to anger, and He restrained Himself. In the situation with my aunt, it took me four days to restrain myself, and I am not proud of it.

Our desire should always be to become more and more godly in our behavior. Here is an example for us to follow:

Our fathers in Egypt understood not nor appreciated Your miracles; they did not [earnestly] remember the multitude of Your mercies nor imprint Your loving kindness [on their hearts], but they were rebellious and provoked the Lord at the sea, even at the Red Sea.

Nevertheless He saved them for His name's sake [to prove the righteousness of the divine character], that He might make His mighty power known.

Psalms 106:7–8

Even though the children of Israel were rebellious and deserved punishment, God forgave them and showed loving kindness to be His own nature. In other words, God is love, and it is not something He turns on and off. He is always the same and never allows the behavior of others to change Him. I allowed my aunt's behavior to quickly change me, but had I taken time to think before I reacted, the entire situation could have been different. I reacted on my emotions, rather than acting on God's Word and following His example. For many years of my life I did the same thing in lots of situations. Anger was pretty much a daily occurrence for me until I was willing to let God change me.

In the next chapter I will discuss how Dave confronted my bad behavior but never mistreated me. That trait of stability and continued willingness to show love to me was one of the major reasons for my desire to change my bad behavior. Had Dave merely become angry and yelled, accused, and threatened me with loss of our relationship, I might not have ever changed. I was at a point in my life where I desperately needed to see love in action, and Dave showed it to me.

Sometimes words are not enough. Saying words of love is common in our society. My father who sexually abused me told me that he loved me. My mother who abandoned me told me that she loved me. Friends who lied to me had told me that they loved me, so words had lost meaning for me. Dave not only told me that he loved me, he showed me the kind of love that God wants to give to others through us. His own love!

Uncontrolled Anger

Uncontrolled anger can quickly turn into rage. Rage is dangerous. In this state, people say and do all kinds of things that can alter the course of their lives. Have you ever heard the statement, "I was so angry that I couldn't even see straight"? That is the way I felt the day I got so angry with my aunt. I realize now that the anger I felt was about more than the situation at hand. I think I had let some resentment build up in me that needed to be resolved, and the incident with her was the straw that broke the camel's back, so to speak.

When we experience other people's anger coming toward us, quite often their anger involves a lot more than the current situation. We might be driving in traffic and have someone get into a rage because we failed to give a proper signal. Their anger is all out of proportion to the offense. We made a simple mistake and they are angry enough to hurt us, but although the anger is being directed at us, it is really not about us at all. It is a buildup of perhaps even years of unresolved issues in their life. Today we frequently hear of a gunman who has walked into a building and shot several people, killing some and injuring others. In a rage, this person started shooting people he did not even know. Why? His rage had built up into a state of uncontrolled violence.

How many people are in prison today because they killed someone in a rage? How many have ruined or seriously damaged relationships because they said terrible, hurtful things in a rage? Think of how many people would have better lives right now if they had been taught how to properly handle the emotion of anger.

The most astonishing act of rage occurred when the Jews were incited to crucify Jesus Who had come to save them and had not done anything wrong. This act of injustice is the most horrible in history, yet God forgave and birthed a plan for our total redemption and restoration. Amazing love!

The only way to avoid rage is to count to 100 when you get angry, or 1,000, or however high you need to count until you calm down. Do that before saying anything or taking any action. I always say, "Let emotions subside and then decide."

Don't Waste Your Emotional Energy on Anger

Getting angry takes a lot of energy. Have you ever noticed how tired you are after a bout of anger? I have, and at my age I finally realized I have no time to waste in my life. Anger is a waste and never does anyone any good unless it is righteous anger, and that is another subject for another chapter. I learned that once I got really angry it took a lot of time for me to calm down, and I finally realized it was better to use some energy controlling anger at the outset than it was to expend all my energy getting angry and trying to calm down. Here is a good piece of advice: If you don't agree with someone, leave the person in God's hands. Ask Him to reveal who is right and who is wrong, and be willing to face the truth if He says it is you.

For too many years I wasted energy arguing with Dave over trivial things that actually made no real difference at all, except that I wanted to be right. But, love gives up its right to be right (1 Cor. 13:5). Being right is not all it is cracked up to be! The energy we waste trying to prove we are right is truly misplaced energy most of the time. Even when I argued with Dave long enough to get him to say, "You're right," I still didn't win, because I had disappointed God with my behavior and been a poor example to all those around me.

Peace gives us power, but anger makes us weak. Let's choose and pursue peace with God, with ourselves, and with man.

For let him who wants to enjoy life and see good days [good—whether apparent or not] keep his tongue free from evil and his lips from guile [treachery, deceit].

Let him turn away from wickedness and shun it, and let him do right. Let him search for peace [harmony; undisturbedness from fears, agitating passions, and moral conflicts] and seek it eagerly. [Do not merely desire peaceful relations with God, with your fellow-men, and with yourself, but pursue, go after them!]

1 Peter 3:10–11

I hope you took the time to read the Scripture above. It caused me to finally see that I could not just pray for peace, but I had to seek it, pursue it, and go after it with all my heart. I had to be willing to make adjustments and adapt to others in order to have peace. I also had to be willing to humble myself as I did the day I called my aunt to apologize, if I truly wanted peace.

What is peace worth to you? If you don't see it as extremely valuable, you will never do what you must do in order to have it. Controlling your anger and learning to forgive generously and quickly are parts of maintaining peace. But always being willing to sacrifice our own desire, especially the desire to be right, is also a daily part of enjoying the peace that God has provided in Jesus Christ. I have discovered that God is much better at vindicating me than I am at trying to vindicate myself. Let God be God in your life, and you will enjoy more peace, too.

The emotion of anger does not have to rule you. It will always be around looking for an opportunity to rear its ugly head, but through the leadership of the Holy Spirit, prayer, and self-control we don't have to give in to it. God's Word states that He will give us power to rule in the midst of our enemies, and as far as I am concerned, anger is an enemy in my life that I refuse to submit to. Do yourself a favor . . . let go of anger, press past it, and enjoy the peace of God.

CHAPTER
3

The Roots of Anger

There are things that we get angry about, but then there are people who are angry about nothing in particular; they are just angry. Sometimes we don't know where our anger comes from. I have had more than one person say to me, "I feel angry a lot and I don't even know why... what is wrong with me?" There is a root to their anger somewhere, and prayer, a little digging, and a lot of facing truth usually bring it out in the open. I have found that God usually shows me what my problem really is if I ask Him. What He shows me is not always what I want to hear, especially if He reveals that I am the problem, but He desires that we face truth in our inner being and let it make us free.

Until I was a middle-aged woman, I had an anger problem. Anytime I didn't get my own way, my temper quickly flared, because I had watched my father behave the same way. Angry people often come from angry families. It is a learned behavior, and until it is confronted, anger will more than likely remain. For example, statistics tell us that many men who batter their wives witnessed the same kind of behavior from their father toward their mother. Even though they may have hated seeing their mother mistreated, they often handle conflict the same way.

My father was frequently violent toward my mother, especially if he had been drinking. He was an angry man, and although we never completely got to the roots of why he was so angry, we did learn that his father was also an angry man who was difficult to please and used anger as a control method in his home. The Bible teaches us that sins and the behavior that accompanies them are inherited from generation to generation unless someone learns to love God and begins to apply His principles to their life (Deut. 5:8–10).

I have seen the cycle of anger and violence in my family broken in my lifetime, and God wants to do the same thing for any person who has a problem with anger. Take some time and think about the home you grew up in. What was the atmosphere?

How did the adults deal with one another in conflict? Was the home filled with pretense or did people relate truthfully and openly? If you happen to be one of the blessed few who grew up in a godly atmosphere, you should thank God because that gave you a head start in life. However, those of us who did not have a good example can recover through the love of God and the truth of His Word.

How to Employ Godly Confrontation

Not only was my father violent, my mother never confronted him. She was timid, so she cowered under his abusive authority. Not only did she not protect herself, but she didn't protect me, either. I learned to despise what I saw as weakness in her, and I determined early in life that I would never be weak or let anyone mistreat me. In an effort to protect myself, I became a controller. I thought if I kept everything and everyone under control then I would not get hurt, but of course my behavior did not work, because it was ungodly. My husband eventually used godly confrontation in our relationship, and although it took time, it helped me change.

Although we are called to peace and should seek and pursue peace, to be afraid to confront people who are mistreating us is not the way to handle conflict. We eventually learned in our home that openness and truth are the best policies at all times. Dave and I have four grown children, and we all spend a lot of time together. There are times when we get angry and things are said that cause conflict, but I am happy to say nobody stays angry for very long. We confront issues, and even if we disagree, we try to disagree agreeably. We know the dangers of strife and are committed to keeping it out of our family. I share this to show that although I grew up in an angry home and initially brought that anger into my own home, that sinful pattern has been broken by the mercy and grace of God, and through obedience to His Word.

Godly confrontation begins by confronting when God leads us to do so and waiting until God leads us to do so. Too much confrontation too soon can just make an angry person angrier. State the problem in a calm and loving way and try to do so in a plain and simple conversation. Confronting anger with anger never works, so it is important that you remain calm during the confrontation.

A soft answer turns away wrath, but grievous words stir up anger.

Proverbs 15:1

A gentle tongue [with its healing power] is
a tree of life, but willful contrariness in it
breaks down the spirit.

Proverbs 15:4

By long forbearance and calmness of spirit a
judge or ruler is persuaded, and soft speech
breaks down the most bonelike resistance.

Proverbs 25:15

Tell the person you are confronting how their
behavior makes you feel, and let them know that it
is unacceptable. Try to keep your tone of voice gentle, but firm. Confirm that you love the person and
want the relationship to be healthy, but that you
will not accept disrespect and abusive treatment
of any type. Don't be at all surprised if the person
doesn't initially accept what you're saying. We usually need time for things to soak into our thinking.
Don't be surprised if the person becomes angry and
begins to accuse you of being the problem. Hold
firm to your decision, pray a lot, and give God time
to work. Quite often the person will come back to
you later and tell you they are sorry and that they
realize you are right.

When Dave confronted me, he told me that he
loved me but was not going to be able to respect

me if I wasn't willing to face my ungodly behavior and let God change me. He told me how my attitude and words toward him made him feel, and he let me know that a lot of damage to his feelings about me would need time to heal. He never mistreated me, nor did he shut me out of his life through silence, but he was firm and determined. At first I rebelled, was very defensive, and tried to tell him all the things that were wrong with him. But eventually I accepted my responsibility and started working with the Holy Spirit toward change. The calm and firm stability that Dave showed all the way through the process was very important, and I believe it is important for anyone who is in a situation that needs to be confronted.

Used and Misused

Abuse means to be misused or to be used in an improper manner. When a father sexually abuses a child, he is using that child in a way that is wrong. When a mother has no loving words of kindness for her children, she is being abusive because her treatment is improper. When a husband beats or batters his wife, he is an abuser. When anyone tries to control another person, it is abuse. God has created us to need love, acceptance, and freedom; these needs are part of our DNA, and we will never function properly without them.

I am overwhelmed when I even try to think about the abuse in our society today. It seems we live in an angry world where most people are like time bombs ready to explode at any moment. People have become very selfish and self-centered, and their anger has grown right along with it. As far as I am concerned, God is the only answer to the problems we face today. We cannot control what the world does, but we can determine not to follow its ways. We should make our decision in favor of God and His ways, and when we do, our lives can become a light that will be a shining example for others. Let us declare, "Choose for yourselves...whom you will serve but as for me and my house we...will serve the Lord" (Joshua 24:15 NKJV).

Any kind of abuse leaves people angry. Are you mad at someone who abused you? Perhaps forgiving them is the beginning of your own healing and turnaround. John 20:23 records Jesus telling His disciples that whoever's sins they retained would be retained; but if they forgave then they would be forgiven. When we refuse to forgive someone who has hurt us, perhaps we keep the sin in us and repeat it ourselves. Many people who have been abused become abusers. At the very least they are angry and unable to change until they completely forgive those who have wounded them. Satan will make sure that someone hurts each of us, hoping that we will live angry lives. But remember Ecclesiastes 7:9, "Anger and vexation lodge in the bosom of fools." We're foolish if we retain the anger we feel when someone hurts us. Do yourself a favor and forgive.

In 1985, Bill Pelke's grandmother, Ruth, was murdered by four teenage girls. She was a wonderful Christian woman who conducted Bible studies in her home. One evening, she opened her door to a group, expecting to teach them God's Word. Instead, the girls entered her home and brutally killed her.

One night in November of 1986, Bill found himself thinking about his grandmother.

*   *   *

On November 2, 1986 [says Pelke], I had been thinking about Nana's life and death. I began to think about her faith. Nana was a devout Christian, and I was raised in a Christian family. I recalled how Jesus said that if we wanted our Father in Heaven to forgive us, we needed to forgive those who had wronged us ... I knew that Jesus was saying that forgiveness should be a habit, a way of life. Forgive, forgive, forgive, and keep on forgiving ... I thought that I should probably try to forgive [Paula Cooper, the fifteen-year-old ringleader] for what she had done to Nana. I figured that maybe someday I would because it would be the right thing to do.

The more I thought about Nana, the more I became convinced that she would have been appalled by the death sentence given to Paula... I also felt she wanted someone in my family to show the same kind of love and compassion. I felt like it fell on my shoulders. Even though I knew forgiveness was the right thing, love and compassion seemed out of the question because Nana had been so brutally murdered. But so convinced that it was what Nana would have wanted and not knowing any other way to achieve it, I begged God to give me love and compassion for Paula Cooper and her family and to do that on behalf of Nana.

It was just a short prayer, but I immediately began to think about how I could write Paula and tell her about the kind of person Nana was and why Nana had let her into her house in the first place. I wanted to share Nana's faith with her.

I realized that the prayer for love and compassion had been answered because I wanted to help Paula and suddenly knew that it would be wrong to execute her. I learned the most powerful lesson of my life that night. That was about the healing power of forgiveness. When my heart was touched with compassion, forgiveness took place. When forgiveness took place, it brought a tremendous healing. It had been a year and a half since Nana's death, and whenever I thought about Nana during that time I always pictured how she died. It was terrible to think about the horrendous death she suffered. But I knew when my heart was touched with compassion and the forgiveness that brought it about, that from that moment on whenever I thought about Nana again, I would no longer picture how she died, but I would picture how she lived, what she stood for, what she believed in, and the beautiful, wonderful person that she was.

Forgiveness does not mean condoning what Cooper did, nor does it mean that there should not be any consequences for her act. It surely did not mean to forgive and forget. I will never forget what happened to Nana, but I can let any desire to get even with Paula go. I can wish for good things to happen to her.

*   *   *

True stories like the one above are very inspiring and they show that we can indeed forgive anyone for anything if we look beyond what has been done to us, to what is going to be the best thing long term for everyone involved. God has been teaching me to not just look at what the offending party has done to me, but to see even more strongly what they have done to themselves and be willing to forgive and pray for them.

Anger Rooted in Perfectionism

If we have unrealistic expectations of ourselves or other people, it can become a root of anger in our lives. A perfectionist is someone who is unable to be satisfied unless things are perfect. Good is never good enough, even excellent is not good enough... things have to be perfect. Unless the perfectionist allows God to bring balance into his or her life, the drive for perfection usually becomes a source of stress and unhappiness.

Life is not perfect and neither are the people in it, yet God has given us the ability to endure whatever comes with a good temper if we are willing to do so.

*   *   *

Lisa's mother was very hard on her, always demanding perfection in everything she did. Even though Lisa was not musically talented, her mother insisted that she learn to play piano and forced her to practice hour after hour. She almost never compli- mented Lisa on anything, and even on rare occa- sions when she did, she also reminded her of the things she still needed to work on. As a result, Lisa has a deep-rooted anger toward herself for what she sees as failure in most everything she does. She is also very legalistic and hard to please in her rela- tionships with her husband and two children. At the age of thirty Lisa has ulcers and irritable bowel syndrome, both of which are negatively affected by the stress that she lives under constantly.

Lisa is currently working with a Christian coun- selor and is making some progress, but it is a daily battle. Life happens every day, and by the end of each day something imperfect has usually hap- pened that Lisa has to consciously decide not to let upset her. She wants to be free from the tyranny of perfectionism, but it will take a while for her mind to be renewed in this area. Lisa will need to learn to act on God's Word, believing what it says, and not to react emotionally to situations based on the memory of her mother's demanding expectations.

Jesus is the only One Who ever did or will meet all the requirements of the law perfectly, and He did it on our behalf so we could be free. Even though we may have a perfect heart attitude toward God and desire perfection, we will manifest some imper- fection as long as we live in natural flesh and blood bodies and have souls that are influenced by everything around us. Through studying God's Word and spending time with Him, we grow toward the mark of perfection, but we must learn to be joyful where we are on the way to where we are going.

Life is about the journey, not the destination.

God's strength is made perfect in our weaknesses. We can be strong, but only in Him. It does us absolutely no good to be angry with ourselves, because we can't be perfect all the time. I have learned to do my best and let God do the rest!

Unmet Needs

We all have legitimate needs, and it is not wrong to expect those in relationship with us to meet some of those needs. However, we must be certain that we look to God first and trust Him to work through others. Most people are drawn toward people who are their opposite. God planned for all of us to be different so that we would need each other. No person has it all, but each of us has a part of what is needed to maintain a healthy balance in life. I am very aggressive and my husband is a bit more laid back. For many years it was the source of arguments between us, but now we see that I often stir him up to action, and he slows me down so I don't act impulsively. Together we are well balanced. You may be in a similar situation, but if you don't see it properly, you will spend your life trying to get someone to give you something they don't even realize you need simply because they are different from you.

I believe that God will meet all our legitimate needs, but He does it through whomever He chooses. I spent lots of time angry with Dave because he didn't understand me, or because he didn't want to spend hours talking with me about our problems. His plan was simple: he wanted to recognize the problem, do what we could do, and then cast our care on God (1 Pet. 5:7). On the other hand, I wanted to figure out what we should do. Dave of course was right, but I not only had a different personality than him, I was also less mature in the area of trusting God.

Over the years I have learned not to keep a mental recording of what I consider to be unmet needs that will eventually turn into a root of anger in my life, but to trust God with each need I have. I know that Dave loves me and that he desires to meet my needs, but the truth is that he just doesn't always see them or know what to do because it is not part of how God put him together. I have learned to look at all the wonderful things Dave does do and not to fixate on the few that he doesn't do.

A grateful heart that is thankful for what it

does have is one that is more successful at avoiding anger and resentment. Be thankful and say so, and aggressively resist anger, because if you don't, it will hurt you more than it will hurt anyone else.

The Need for Correction

In those early years of our marriage, I actually needed Dave to correct me, even though I didn't like it initially. He did it because he loved me and wanted our relationship to be healthy. The Bible teaches us that a true friend will wound us with blows of correction when needed. It is often easier on us to simply ignore wrong behavior because we don't want to deal with the drama that ensues when we do bring correction, but genuine concern for the other person won't permit us to do that.

Children not only need love and affection, they need correction. If a child is not corrected, they become rebellious and disrespectful. A large percentage of men and women in prison testify that their parents never corrected them properly. Our daughter Sandra and her husband Steve have twin girls who are currently eight years old. Steve and Sandra are very good parents showing lots of love, but they are also firm in their correction. Just to show how children respond to a good balance of love and correction, let me share with you a note my granddaughter Angel wrote to her mom while she was spending the evening alone in her room being corrected for telling a lie.

"Dear Mom, I love you very much, I care for you and I want you to know that I love you very, very, very, very much."

Angel knew that being corrected was the right thing for her and that it was an act of love from her parents. She wrote a similar note to her dad.

God's Word tells us that He chastises (corrects) those whom He loves (Heb. 12:6). He sets the example He wants us to follow with our children. Give your children a lot of love, plenty of forgiveness, and confrontation and correction at the right time.

Many roots of anger take hold in our lives, and perhaps the root of your anger hasn't been addressed here. Ask God to show you why you are angry. When you get angry, think not only about what triggered that anger, but see if you're reminded of other times in your life when you felt similarly. Is there a pattern?

While understanding the root of a problem doesn't by itself solve the problem, it can bring insight and understanding, which is a great first step toward healing.

We have many needs in our life, and when those needs go unmet they can cause us to have anger issues, but the truth will make us free. Just realizing where our anger stems from is sufficient truth to begin the process of healing.

CHAPTER
4

The Roots of Jealousy

Wrath is cruel and anger is an overwhelming flood, but who is able to stand before jealousy?

Proverbs 27:4

Jealousy is a terrible thing. It is often referred to as "the green-eyed monster," and so it is because it devours the life of the one who permits it in his heart. According to Proverbs 27:4 it is worse than wrath and anger. Jealousy is such a huge problem that I feel it deserves a chapter of its own.

*   *   *

Jennifer spent her life comparing herself with her sister Jacque; they were twins but not identical. Jacque was born first and had a bubbly, outgoing personality; whereas Jennifer was shy and quiet. Instead of finding and developing her abilities, Jennifer adopted the lazy trait of being jealous of what her sister could do. I say that jealousy is laziness because it takes no effort at all to sit around feeling sorry for ourselves and resenting others who have what we want. Yes, Jacque was talented in many ways, but actually Jennifer was, too; however, her bitterness toward her sister prevented her from even seeing her own talents. As the years went by, what could have been and should have been a close, loving relationship between sisters turned into a competition on Jennifer's part. The jealousy that was always present in Jennifer's heart cast a dark shadow on her teenage years. Jacque was so happy and full of life that she barely noticed the bitterness in her sister's attitude, and that infuriated Jennifer even more. She wanted her sister to notice how unhappy she was, and furthermore, she wanted her to be unhappy, too.

By the time they were adults and had children of their own, Jacque did realize there was a problem, but no matter how hard she tried to develop a close relationship with Jennifer, it never worked. They were socially polite to one another, but the rift was always present. This angry undercurrent could be felt by everyone, and the entire family suffered from one girl's insecurity and jealousy.

How does a cycle like this even get started in people's lives? Satan is always lurking around trying to find a way to bring strife between people, especially family members. Perhaps Jennifer's parents complimented Jacque for a job well done on the same day they had corrected Jennifer for a bad judgment call, and Satan used the situation to sow a seed of self-doubt and bitterness. There may be a thousand different scenarios, but the result is always the same. When we live in strife rooted in jealousy, we forfeit the peace, joy, and abundant life that God desires us to have.

The tenth commandment that God gave Moses to bring to the people is "You shall not covet your neighbor's house, your neighbor's wife, or his manservant, or his maidservant or his ox, or his donkey, or anything that is your neighbor's" (Exod. 20:17). The commandment means we should not envy or be jealous of anything that anyone else has. Jealousy is a sin of the heart. It is an attitude that feeds strife and anger, and it brings division. God wants us to be happy for the blessings of others, and until we can do that, we usually don't obtain what we desire. Or if we do obtain what we want, we are not able to be happy and content with it because

we will always see someone else who has more than
we do and find ourselves unhappy again.

The apostle Paul said that he coveted no man's
silver or gold or costly garments (Acts 20:33). He
was content to do what God had called him to do
and to be who God had created him to be. Contentment is a blessed place to dwell, but one that
few find and remain in for very long. Paul knew a
secret. He knew that he was in God's will and that
God would provide whatever was right for him at
the right time. He was not a passive man without
desires, but he was a man of faith who had complete trust in the goodness and wisdom of God.

John the Baptist was another man of God who
apparently had no jealousy. The Bible says in John
3:25–27 that a controversy arose between the disciples of John and those of Jesus regarding the
doctrine of purification. John had been baptizing
people and now Jesus' disciples had come along and
were baptizing, and people were flocking to Jesus.
We see the root of jealousy causing anger and con-
tention. When the report came to John he said, "A
man can receive nothing (he can claim nothing,
he can take unto himself nothing) except as it has
been granted to him from heaven. (A man must be
content to receive the gift which is given him from
heaven; there is no other source.)"

When I struggled in my own life with jealousy

and felt angry because I didn't always have what others had, these Scriptures really helped me. I began to realize that if I trusted God, then I had to trust that what He gave me was right for me and that it was very wrong to be jealous of what He (God) had given someone else.

God knows us better than we know ourselves, and we can enjoy contentment if we trust that in His goodness He will never withhold any good thing from us at the right time.

The apostle James tells us that strife (discord and feuds) and conflicts (quarrels and fightings) originate from the desires we have that are ever warring in our body members. We are jealous and covet what others have, and our desires go unfulfilled. Then we begin to hate, which is murder as far as the heart is concerned. James states that people burn with envy and anger and are not able to obtain the gratification and contentment and the happiness they seek. Then James says something that became a pivotal verse in my own life:

You do not have, because you do not ask.
James 4:2b

These few words freed me from the frustration of not having what I wanted and being jealous of others who did have it. I saw clearly that if I wanted something, I was to ask God for it and trust that if it was the right thing for me, He would give it in His own time. With God, there's plenty to go around. He may not always give us what someone else has, but He will always provide for us abundantly if we trust Him and His timing in our lives.

I further learned that if God did not give me what I asked for, it was not because He was holding out on me, but that He had something better in mind and that I should be content to wait for it. Prior to understanding "You do not have because you do not ask," my heart was full of strife because I was operating in works of the flesh and trying to make my own ideas and plans work. I decided what I wanted and behaved as if God was obligated to give it to me. I had a very childish and selfish attitude. Jealousy is indeed cruel.

Hatred That Became Violent

King Saul was so angry that he tried repeatedly to kill David, and his anger was a result of jealousy that was rooted in fear of losing his position to David (1 Sam. 18:6–12). Saul was so enraged that at one point he threw his spear at his son Jonathan because he and David were friends (1 Sam. 20:30–34). We can readily see that his anger and jealousy turned into rage that made him a violent man.

There are many biblical examples, but we don't want to read the account of other people's lives and ignore the problem in our own. Are you jealous of anyone? Do you feel angry when someone else does better than you in sports, business, or any other area in your life? All too often we see anger rear its ugly head during sports competitions. We all want to win, but when we want to win so bad that we become angry with those who do better than us, we are wrong. I remember playing volleyball on a church league and watching Christians behave in a very ungodly manner due to competition. This green-eyed monster of jealousy is after everyone, so we must beware.

If you find yourself jealous of anyone for any reason, you may as well do yourself a favor and get over it, because being jealous will never get you anything but misery. God has a unique and special plan for each one of us. We are all different, but equally valuable, and knowing that helps us be content and satisfied with who we are and what we have.

Different but Not Less

All the comparisons and competition in our society are very tragic and the root cause of much anger and division. Just because we are different from other people, it does not mean that we are less— or more—than they are. Everything is valuable in its own way. My hands are very different from my feet, yet they are not jealous of each other. They work together in a beautiful way, each performing the function God has designed for them. God wants us to do the same thing. He wants us to see our individual beauty and value and never feel inferior because we are different from someone else. I heard a minister put it this way: "We must learn to be comfortable in our own skin."

Anger reflects feelings of inferiority. We need to relate to other people as equals, with no need to feel better than them and never feeling inferior. Jesus is the great equalizer! Through Him we are all equal. He said there is no more male nor female, Jew nor Greek, slave nor free, but we are all one in Him (Gal. 3:28). Our value is not in what we can do, but in who we are and Who we belong to. We belong to God, and our looks, talents, and other abilities come from Him. A short man cannot make himself one inch taller by worrying or being jealous of someone who is taller than he is. What he can do is strive to be the best he can be in life and never compare himself to anyone else.

Zacchaeus was a man who was short in stature. When he heard that Jesus was passing by, he really wanted to see Him, but he knew he would never be able to see over the huge crowd because he was short. Zacchaeus could have gotten depressed because of his size. He could have even considered it a handicap and fallen into self-pity and passivity. But Zacchaeus did neither. Instead he ran ahead of the crowd and climbed a tree so he could see clearly. When Jesus passed by, He saw Zacchaeus in the tree and told him to come down because He was going to his house for dinner (Luke 19:1–6). This is one of my favorite stories in the Bible because I see that Zacchaeus's good attitude was pleasing to Jesus. He liked it so much that He spent special time with him. Zacchaeus could have missed the whole event had he been angry because he was short in stature.

If you are angry right now about anything you are not and wish you were, I strongly recommend that you learn a lesson from Zacchaeus. Do the best you can with what you have to work with, and God will always make up the difference and promote you in life. Realize that God carefully created you with His own hand in your mother's womb, and He does not make mistakes. Everything God made is good, and that includes you.

I suggest you take a few moments and make a list of anything you don't like about your physical appearance or abilities. After you do that, ask God to forgive you for not liking what He chose for you, tear the list up, throw it away, and ask God to help you be fully and completely you.

Until I learned better, I wanted my voice to be softer, my legs to be thinner, and my hair to be thicker. When I saw women who had what I wanted, I could feel myself shutting them out of my life. When we are jealous of another person it prevents us from enjoying them. I resented those women who had what I wanted, and I felt inferior to them. The truth is that they probably disliked things about themselves, too, and may have even been jealous of something I had that they didn't.

Jealousy is one of the tools that Satan uses to bring division between people, and it is a total waste of time on our part because it does no good and certainly doesn't help us get what we think we want.

One of the reasons I am writing this book is to help you make the decision not to keep wasting your time doing things that produce no good fruit. We are truly doing ourselves a favor when we refuse to be jealous of others and simply trust God's love for us.

*   *   *

The story of Joseph in the Bible is one of amazing victory. Joseph was the baby boy in the family and favored by his father. I don't think his father loved him more than his brothers, he just loved him differently. Joseph was the baby, and babies usually tend to get a little more attention in every family. His brothers were jealous, and their jealousy made them angry enough to sell Joseph to slave traders and then tell their father Joseph was killed by a wild animal. Joseph spent many years in very unfavorable circumstances, including being imprisoned for thirteen years for a crime he did not commit. But because he had a good attitude, he was always promoted in whatever task he was assigned. God always promotes us in life if we trust Him and don't let emotions like fear, inferiority, anger, and jealousy rule us. Joseph could have responded to his brothers' anger with anger of his own. He could have let that anger make him bitter and it could have ruined his life, but he did not let his brothers' bad decision rule him.

Are you letting a bad decision someone else made keep you angry? If you are, then you're being foolish because you do have another choice. You can do yourself a favor and move beyond what they did. We cannot always change what others do, but we don't have to let their choices control our behavior. God has given each of us free choice. We can choose life or death in every situation. Free choice also means that we have responsibility, so in reality if I am unhappy it is my own fault because I can choose not to be.

If we read the entire story of Joseph in the Bible we learn that eventually his family came to him very repentant for how they had treated him, and he graciously helped them during a time of famine. Not only did Joseph refuse to become angry and bitter, he was quick to forgive his brothers who had done a truly terrible thing to him. The person who forgives is always greater than the one who is jealous and angry. Only small-minded people let jealousy and anger determine their destiny.

Jesus Is Our Healer

We learn in Scripture that Jesus came to heal, but His healing does not always come through miraculous means. Healing often comes through following the Healer's prescription for a healthy life. In other words, if we do what Jesus has taught us to do, we will not only have more joy, but we will also be healthier.

A calm and undisturbed mind and heart are the life and health of the body, but envy, jealousy, and wrath are like rottenness of the bones.

Proverbs 14:30

This is what I call a WOW Scripture. Peace promotes healing, but turmoil, envy, jealousy, and wrath can cause poor health. Doctors tell us that 80 percent of all physical symptoms are induced by stress and that good health is impossible unless excess stress is minimized or removed. Anger leaves me feeling very stressed, and I am sure it does the same thing to you. Jealousy is anger about what another person has that we don't have, and it has a negative effect on our health.

Any kind of anger, no matter what it is rooted in, causes stress, and stress causes illness. When I experienced the incident with my aunt mentioned earlier, I remember that I felt completely worn out after a couple of days of being angry. I was aching in various places, had a headache, and was very tired. Anger is not God's will, and our bodies don't function well with it.

I went to church with a woman who told me that she suffered greatly with arthritis for many years until she was able to forgive a family member who had done her a great injustice. Once she forgave, her pain gradually diminished over a few days and never returned. I am not suggesting that if you have arthritis then you also have unforgiveness. I am not saying that if you have headaches it is due to jealousy. But I do suggest that you search your heart and let any of these negative emotions go before asking God for healing. I firmly believe that negative emotions are the root cause of much illness and that releasing them can help promote healing and energy in our lives.

Jesus said, "I am the Way." When we follow His ways we will have the best life possible. When we disobey His principles we can expect trouble in every area of our life.

Contentment

I keep a journal that I write in every morning, and as I look over the past couple of years' entries, I see several entries that just say, "I am content." Being able to say that means a lot to me, because I wasted lots of years being discontent. There was always something else I thought I had to have in order to be fully satisfied. The apostle Paul stated that he had learned "how to be content (satisfied to the point I am was not disturbed)" no matter what his circumstances were (Phil. 4:11). I do believe that contentment is something we must learn because every human being is born with discontentment. It is in our flesh and will never be quiet unless we stop feeding it.

Are you content? If not, please pursue contentment because it is a wonderful place to be. Being content doesn't mean that we don't want things, but it means we are content with what we have until God sees fit to give us something else. A parent feels hurt when his or her child is discontent no matter what that child has. We see what we do for them, but they see what others have that they don't. They want the latest, greatest smart phone, the newest computer, the name-brand tennis shoes, and on and on. We want them to be thankful for what they have. We don't mind being asked for things, but we don't want to be pressured by a bad attitude that is never satisfied. If we feel that way toward our children, how does God view our discontentment? I don't think it motivates Him to get us what we think we want, but it may motivate Him to make us wait longer until we learn what is truly important in life.

Our thoughts feed our feelings, so if you feel discontent, the way to get over it is to change your thinking. Think about what you *do* have instead of what you don't have. Think about God's wisdom and goodness and remind yourself that He has heard your prayers and will do what is best for you in His perfect timing. Every time you see someone being blessed, especially if they have something you want and don't have yet, thank God for blessing them. Do it in obedience to God, and joy will be released in your heart.

My Jealous Friend

I had a friend who was jealous of what God gave me, and it made me very uncomfortable. For example, someone gave me a beautiful ring as a gift, and my friend's comment was, "I wish someone would give me a ring." Part of being a good friend is to genuinely share in each other's joy. Because of her attitude, when I was blessed after that, I felt it was best not to tell her. I tried to guard my comments so I wouldn't say anything that would feed her jealousy and insecurity. Being with her became too much work for me, and sadly, I eventually started avoiding her.

Out of the heart the mouth speaks. We can hear jealousy come out of the mouth of others, and we can also hear it come out of us if we truly listen. I am determined to do myself a favor and not be jealous of anyone, and I hope you will join me in this holy pursuit. Greed, envy, and jealousy all cause anger, and anger does not promote the righteousness that God desires.

CHAPTER
5

Masking Anger

Because anger is generally viewed as being unacceptable behavior, we find ways to hide it from others and even from ourselves. We mask anger with other behaviors. A mask might be worn to hide something that is unpleasant to look at, to keep people from seeing what is behind the mask. Masks are worn at costume parties to keep people from knowing who we truly are, or to trick them into thinking we are someone or something we are not. It is time to take the masks off and face anger for what it is and deal with it according to God's will.

Let's take a look at some of the masks we wear when we are angry.

The cold-shoulder mask is a very common mask of anger. We pretend that we are not angry but become cold (no warmth or emotion) in our dealings with the individual we are supposedly not angry with. I recall many times in my life praying what I call "the official I-forgive-you prayer," but remaining distant and cool toward the one I had told God I was forgiving. As a Christian, I know I am not supposed to stay angry and that it is in fact dangerous to do so for reasons I will discuss later in this book. Wanting to do the right thing, I prayed saying, "God, I forgive _____ for hurting me; help me get over the pain I feel." I meant what I said, but at that time I did not realize that I had to add obedient action to obedient prayer. God wanted me to take the next step and treat the person warmly as if nothing had happened, but I was not willing to do that.

The Bible says in 1 Peter 4:8 that our love should be fervent (red-hot). Cold love is never acceptable to God, because it is a pretense of the real thing He desires. Real love must be genuine, strong, and warm, not cool and distant. According to Scripture, the love of Christians will grow cold because of the multiplied wickedness and lawlessness in the land (Matt. 24:12). As the end of time draws near and we look forward to the second coming of Jesus

Christ, we must aggressively resist letting our love toward others become cold and lifeless.

Because I am a responsible person, I always do my duty even when my responsibility is toward someone I am angry with. I still meet my obligation but have often done it coldly, showing no genuine affection or kindness. For example, there were times when I was angry with my entire family for disappointing me in some way and yet I still cooked and served their dinner. I did my duty, but mechanically and coldly. If anyone asked me if something was wrong, I said, "No, I am fine." I am sure you are familiar with this type of behavior. It is one of the ways we pretend all is well, but we are hiding behind a mask that we hope deceives others into thinking we are behaving properly.

I can always feel it when someone is doing something for me out of duty rather than desire, and I must say that I dislike it very much. I would just as soon they did not do it at all because I can feel the pretense. I am sure others can also feel it when I behave that way, and I have made a commitment to be genuine, rather than phony. I think it would be better to tell someone that I am angry and need some time to get over it, than it is to pretend nothing is wrong while I seethe with anger inside.

Shutting People Out of Our Lives

The mask of avoidance—We have many ways of shutting people out of our lives. The silent treatment is one of those ways. When we are angry, sometimes we blow up and sometimes we clam up. We tell ourselves and others that we are not angry, and yet we refuse to talk to the one we are supposedly not angry with. If conversation is necessary, we say as little as possible. We murmur, grunt, nod, or do anything other than talk normally. There have been times when I have been angry and felt that my mouth was cemented shut. Even when I knew I needed to talk to the person and stop acting childish, it took all my willpower to part my lips and speak.

We can shut people out by avoiding touching them. I have been angry with Dave and literally scooted so far onto my side of the bed to keep from touching him that I felt as if I were sleeping on the outer seam of the mattress. I have spent the entire night cold because I refused to ask him for any of the covers. This was foolish behavior on my part because Dave slept great while I was miserable all night! I remember those times and how distressed I was in my soul, and I am extremely glad that with God's help I have grown past that kind of behavior.

Have you ever been angry and avoided being in the room with the one you are angry with? If they come into the room where you are, you find a reason to leave. If they want to watch television, you want to go to bed, but if they want to go to bed, you want to stay up and watch television. When they want to eat, you are not hungry. If they want to go for a walk or take a ride, you have a headache. These are all masks we wear, acting as if everything is fine when in reality our behavior exposes the truth.

I have refused to bring Dave coffee in the morning, cook the food I know he likes, or call him to tell him things I normally would, all the while telling myself I had forgiven him for some offense. These types of behavior keep us in bondage, but obedience to God's Word will set us free.

Some preachers or pastors use their pulpits and sermons to address issues they are angry about with their congregation or specific members of the congregation. They mask their anger in a sermon that they supposedly got from God. A man and woman I know who were pastors got a divorce due to the husband's unfaithfulness. The woman continued preaching, but for almost two years all her sermons were about people who control and manipulate us. She preached about not allowing people to use you, how to have safe relationships, and other things along these lines. Everything she shared with the congregation seemed to be something out of her own situation. She was preaching out of her pain rather than preaching as directed by the Holy Spirit. She repeatedly told me she had forgiven her husband and was moving on, but I rarely ever spoke with her that she did not bring up what he had done to her. As long as we are still talking about our wounds, we have not gotten over them. We may pretend that we have, but in reality we haven't.

The Bible states that the heart is deceitful above all else and that it is difficult for one to know their own heart (Jer. 17:9). Self-deception is a way of hiding from the truth. I can tell myself that I am no longer angry and that I have forgiven, but if I treat a person coldly, refuse to talk to them, avoid them, and continue talking about what they have done to hurt me, then I have not forgiven and I am hurting myself more than anyone else.

Misusing Scripture

The Scripture mask—I believe we can even use Scripture to vent our anger on people. A good example is Ephesians 4:15, which says, "Speak the truth in love." This verse is often used as a cover-up to express our own anger or disappointment with individuals as we tell them the truth about what they have done. Are we telling them the truth for their benefit or ours? Are we speaking the truth in love because of genuine concern for them, or have we found a new supposedly God-approved method of telling people off?

I have been the victim of a few people who were "speaking the truth in love" to me. However, what they said hurt me and gave me a problem to deal with. I recall a woman who said, "Joyce, I need to tell you the truth about something," and I could tell from her tone that I might not like what she was about to say. She went on to tell me how I had offended her in one of my sermons and how terribly hurt she was, but then assured me that she had forgiven me. This of course was ridiculous and she was self-deceived, because had she truly forgiven me, there would have been no need to bring it up. She merely used a Scripture to vent her anger.

As I said previously, there are times when we need to confront others about their behavior, but we need to make sure we are doing it for their benefit as well as ours. We especially need to be sure that our confrontation is God-ordained and not merely our own decision. Some people don't like confrontation, but it was rarely a problem for me. As a matter of fact, I had to learn to not confront unless God wanted me to. There are times when God wants us to deal with something ourselves and keep it to ourselves without saying anything to anyone. Just because someone hurts my feelings doesn't mean I have to tell them. It may be a greater and godlier decision to "cover" their offense and let it go.

Our anger can become like a drama. We act it out in many ways and, sad to say, often fool ourselves into thinking we are not angry people. Ask God to show you if you are masking your anger in any way, and if you are, take off your masks and begin to let God bring healing into your life. Once again let me remind you, "The truth will make you free."

My Life Is a Mess Because of Anger

A Bag of Nails

Once upon a time there was a little boy with a bad temper. His father gave him a bag of nails and told him that every time he lost his temper, he should hammer a nail in the fence. The first day the boy had driven thirty-seven nails into the fence. But gradually, the number of daily nails dwindled down. He discovered it was easier to hold his temper than to drive those nails into the fence. Finally, the first day came when the boy didn't lose his temper at all. He proudly told his father about it, and the father suggested that the boy now pull out one nail for each day he was able to hold his temper. The days passed and the young boy was finally able to tell his father that all the nails were gone. The father took his son by the hand and led him to the fence. "You have done well, my son, but look at the holes in the fence. The fence will never be the same. When you say things in anger, they leave a scar just like this one. You can put a knife in a man and draw it out, it won't matter how many times you say 'I'm sorry,' the wound is still there."

What are the results of long-term anger? Every area of our lives is damaged by it. Body, soul, and spirit are affected adversely. Our health and relationships are damaged. The possibility of a successful future is hindered by anger because anger alters our personality, and angry people often find it difficult to keep a job. We can never be the person God intends us to be if we remain angry. I believe all of society is affected by our anger, but we are affected more than anyone and that is why I am repeatedly saying, "Do yourself a favor and forgive." Remember, even if your anger is the result of a justifiable offense, you're still not helping yourself or solving the situation by staying angry.

One man's tombstone read:

Here lies Dirty Dan.
He was an angry man.

Always crabby, always mad.
He died young, and we're glad.

Everyone is glad when an angry person is no longer around, because they place stress on all of us. My father was an angry man for most of his life, and his anger created an atmosphere that was stressful to live in. My mother has said several times since he died how much she enjoys just sitting in her apartment and being peaceful and quiet. My mother stayed with my dad because she was committed to the marriage, but the stress she experienced damaged her health, and the anger my father had damaged his.

Stress, especially long-term stress, breaks down every organ in the body. Blood pressure, heart, and stomach are affected. Angry people age quicker than peaceful people: severe headaches, colon problems, anxiety, or immune disorders—actually, the list is endless. The truth is that angry people often die sooner than those who are quick to forgive.

I believe it is time to face the truth about anger and deal with it. If you are an angry person, make a decision to get to the root cause and work with the Holy Spirit toward freedom from it. Don't mask it or ignore it. Face it squarely and call it what it is. To say "I am angry" doesn't sound attractive, but admitting it is the first step toward overcoming it.

This is something that you must do for yourself. Others will benefit from the positive effects of you no longer being angry, but nobody benefits as much as you do.

I was thirty-two years old before I was even open to facing the truth of my past. I was abused sexually by my father. He molested me from the time I can remember until I was old enough for him to have sex with me, and the last five years I lived at home, he raped me approximately two hundred times. I know that sounds shocking and it is, but facing that truth squarely was one of the things I had to do in order to get past it. (My detailed testimony is available on DVD from our ministry.)

After I moved away from home at the age of eighteen years, I assumed that the problem was behind me. Of course I was bitter and hated my father with vehemence, but I had no idea how much it was hurting me. When I began my journey of facing truth and forgiving, I truly had no idea how much it would help me in the long run. Initially I just wanted to obey God and forgive. Angry people cannot love properly, because what is in us always comes out of us in some way. All my relationships were suffering due to my anger and resentment, but I didn't know it. My anger was deeply rooted in my soul. It was in my thinking, my emotions, my words, and all of my actions because it was part of me. Anger had been with me so long that I didn't recognize it for what it was.

As I studied God's Word, the Holy Spirit began showing me the problems that I had. Prior to that, all I thought about was what others had done to me, and it never occurred to me that my reaction to their actions was anything I even needed to look at. I felt justified in hating and resenting not only my dad who hurt me, but the people who could have helped me and didn't. How could God ask me or others who have been abused to forgive such unspeakable offenses? He does it because He knows it is the best thing for us. God has a plan for our complete restoration, and anything He asks us to do is because He loves us and has our best interest in mind. He will give us the grace to forgive even though it may seem impossible to us if we are willing to obey Him.

When I talk to you about getting beyond anger and making forgiveness a lifestyle, I am doing it from experience. I not only know how difficult it is to do, but I also know how valuable it is to you once you do it. Therefore, I strongly encourage you to not just read this book so you can conquer another book to add to your "books I've read" list, but read it with an open heart in readiness to apply what you read to your own life.

God has a wonderful life prearranged and made

ready for every person, and if we will cooperate with Him by doing what He asks us to do, we will enjoy that life. If we don't, then we will miss it. God will still love us, but we will miss the joy of His good plan. Do yourself a favor and refuse to miss one good thing that God has arranged for you.

CHAPTER
6

Who Are You Angry At?

As we have discussed, we are often angry with those who have hurt or wounded us. We may feel anger toward those who hurt us long ago and those who hurt us on a daily basis. We are angry about injustice, and our soul screams that it isn't fair! But others are not always the source of our anger. The Bible tells us to be at peace with God, ourselves, and our fellow man (1 Pet. 3:10–11).

I Am Mad at Me

Are you angry at yourself? Many people are. In fact, it is probably safe to say that more people have a rift with themselves than those who are totally at peace with themselves. Why? As we have discussed previously, we have unrealistic expectations, and we compare ourselves with others and feel that we don't measure up. We may have deep-rooted shame for something we either did or something that was done to us. We feel so guilty that we become angry at ourselves. Most often, though, people are angry with themselves because they do things they don't approve of and they don't know how to receive God's forgiveness and power to overcome their unacceptable behavior.

Believe it or not, the first step toward peace with yourself is to squarely look your sin in the face and call it what it is. Ignoring or making excuses for bad behavior is never the pathway to freedom. As long as we are doing sinful things, we can never have genuine peace with ourselves. Even if we have failed to recognize and take responsibility for our sin, it still bothers us.

Receiving God's Forgiveness

Once we do admit that we are sinners, we must repent of our sins. That means that we are not only heartily sorry for our sins, but we are willing to turn away from them. Living in sin is a low level of life, but when we repent we return to the highest place that God desires for us. The penthouse is the highest apartment in an apartment building. It is the one on the very top floor. When we repent, we return to the highest place God has for us—the place of peace and joy in His righteousness.

Fully admitting and taking responsibility for our sin can be difficult in the beginning. We have usually had a lifetime of blaming and making excuses, so we find it difficult to merely say, "I am guilty. I have committed sin." But all have sinned and come short of the glory of God, so to say we have sinned puts us in no worse position than any other human being on the planet.

> If we say we have no sin [refusing to admit that we are sinners], we delude and lead ourselves astray, and the Truth [which the Gospel presents] is not in us [does not dwell in our hearts].
>
> If we [freely] admit that we have sinned and confess our sins, He is faithful and just [true to His own nature and promises] and will forgive our sins [dismiss our lawlessness] and [continuously] cleanse us from all unrighteousness [everything not in conformity to His will in purpose, thought, and action].
>
> *1 John 1:8–9*

There is a great deal about these Scriptures that I love and that bring comfort to me, but I especially like that He *continuously* cleanses us from all sin. I believe that shows us that as long as we walk with God, quickly admitting our sins and repenting of them regularly, He is always cleansing us. The Bible says that Jesus is sitting at the right hand of God continuously making intercession for us, and I suppose that is because we continuously need it. That also gives me comfort.

He cleanses us from *all* unrighteousness, and if we believe that and receive His forgiveness by faith, we can get over being angry with ourselves. There is no sin you or I can commit that is beyond God's ALL. When He says all, He means all!

Just as all have sinned and come short of the glory of God, all are justified and put into right relationship with Him through the redemption that is provided in Jesus Christ (Rom. 3:23–24). All includes you and me!

God's forgiveness is a free gift, and there is nothing we can do with a free gift except receive it and be grateful. I think we often ask for forgiveness but still fail to receive it. After you ask God to forgive you for something you have done wrong, tell Him that you receive His gift and wait in His presence for a moment while you actually take into your consciousness how wonderful that gift really is.

Don't Be Afraid of Sin

Anytime we are afraid of a thing, we give it power over us, so for that reason I am encouraging you not to be afraid of sin. The apostle Paul wrote that sin no longer has any power over us if we believe that when Christ died we died and when He was raised we were raised to a new life lived for Him (Rom. 6:5–8). Jesus had completely taken care of the problem of sin. Not only does He completely and continuously forgive us, but He has sent His Holy Spirit to convict us of sin in our daily life and to strengthen us against it.

When we initially realize we are sinners and in need of a Savior and we receive Jesus Christ as the only One Who can meet that need, we are on our way to a new life and a new lifestyle. Whereas we once sinned and didn't even really care, now after having received the Spirit of God into our hearts, we become very aware of sin and will spend our lives resisting and avoiding it. We do it gladly as a service to God, and we totally trust the Holy Spirit to help us. Temptation will come to all, and we can be assured that God will never allow any temptation to overtake us that is not common to man (1 Cor. 10:13). In other words, our temptations are no worse than anyone else's, and we are to believe that they are not beyond our ability to resist. God never allows more to come than what we can bear, and with every temptation He also provides a way out. That is really good news! We don't have to fear temptation, because the greater One lives in us, giving us divine strength to resist, if we will only trust Him and ask for His help.

People give in to temptation when they try to resist on their own, or when they erroneously believe that they cannot resist. I hear people make ridiculous statements like "If I eat one chocolate chip cookie, I just can't resist eating the whole package," or "I know sugar is hurting me, but I cannot resist eating chocolate every day." I say these statements are ridiculous because they are founded on lies that we believe. Satan tells us that we are weak and cannot resist even the simplest of temptations, but God tells us that we're strong in Him and nothing is beyond our ability to resist. What we choose to believe is the deciding factor in whether we will cave in to sin or defeat it. Take some time and ask yourself if you are believing things that don't agree with God's Word. Do you believe you can resist temptation through the power of the Holy Spirit and by exercising the fruit of self-control, or do you believe there are some temptations that you just cannot resist? What we believe is what becomes our reality; therefore, it is vital for each of us to know

that what we believe is the truth and not a decep-
tion from the devil.

The apostle Paul prayed that the church would
know and believe in the power that was available
to them through Jesus Christ. If you are a believer
in Jesus Christ, you have power and you can resist
temptation!

We all sin, and as long as we are in flesh-and-
bone bodies with souls that are not completely
renewed, we will need forgiveness, but we don't
have to fear sin. Look carefully at this Scripture:

> My little children, I write you these things so
> that you may not violate God's law and sin.
> But if anyone should sin, we have an Advo-
> cate (One Who will intercede for us) with the
> Father—[it is] Jesus Christ [the all] righteous
> [upright, just, Who conforms to the Father's
> will in every purpose, thought, and action].
>
> And He [that same Jesus Himself] is the
> propitiation [the atoning sacrifice] for our
> sins, and not for ours alone but also for [the
> sins of] the whole world.
>
> *1 John 2:1–2*

These Scriptures are shockingly wonderful.
When I first became aware of them it was a time
in my life when I struggled daily trying to do

everything right so I could feel good about myself and believe that God wasn't angry with me. Obviously, my thinking was wrong, but it was my reality at the time. When I saw that I should simply get up every day and do my best and believe God would take care of any mistakes I did make, I felt as if a huge weight had been lifted off my shoulders.

These Scriptures say that Jesus is the propitiation for our sin. What does that mean? He is the appeasement for God's anger toward sin.

God does hate sin, but He does not hate sinners. When a woman is very angry with her husband because he is disrespectful toward her, and he sends her three dozen red roses with an apology, the roses become the appeasement for her anger. She forgives him and all is well again. Jesus is like our roses that are presented to God when He is angry toward our sin. He is our propitiation, and God forgives us because of Christ. There is nothing we have that would suffice as an appeasement and nothing we can do to make up for or sacrifice for our sins, but Jesus is the perfect sacrifice and He is our substitute. He is our Advocate Who takes our place before God, and we are forgiven because of our faith in Him.

Believing these truths is the first step toward freedom from sin and anger toward yourself because of sin. When I sin I often feel disappointed in myself and pray that I will do better, but I no longer get angry at myself, because I know that is not the will of God and that it will serve no purpose at all.

Dealing Harshly with Sin

In addition to knowing how to quickly and completely receive God's forgiveness when we sin, we also need to aggressively resist sin and deal with it harshly. The fact that God is willing to forgive us does not mean that we can freely sin and think it is not a problem. God knows our heart, and no person's heart is right if they don't hate sin and do all they can to avoid it.

The Romans asked Paul if they should continue in sin in order that God's grace (goodness and forgiveness) might overflow and abound. Paul answered by saying, "How can we who died to sin live in it any longer?" (Rom. 6:1–2). Paul reminded them that when they received Christ, they made a decision to no longer have an active relationship with sin. Sin never dies; it will always be alive and well on planet Earth, but *we* die to sin. God gives us a new heart and His Spirit, and that means we have a new "want to." We spend our lives resisting sin, simply because we no longer want to sin. That being our attitude, when we do make mistakes, God is ever ready to forgive us.

If you are a genuine Christian, I can assure you that you don't get out of bed in the morning looking for ways to sin and get away with it. You do all you can do to live a life that is pleasing to God.

If we don't maintain a bold, aggressive attitude toward sin, then our own heart will condemn us and we will end up angry with ourselves. The Bible teaches us to deal very harshly, even violently with sin. In Matthew 18:8–9 we are instructed that if our eye offends us, we should pluck it out, and if our hand offends us, we should cut it off.

I don't believe this is something we should take literally, but we should see that God is telling us to have an aggressive attitude toward sin, cutting it off wherever we find it in our lives. If a magazine arrives in your home with pictures of women scantily dressed (which happens often) and your eye begins to see and even enjoy it, quickly rip the magazine up and put it in the trash. Deal with it quickly. Don't ever flirt with sin. There are literally dozens of examples I could cite, but I will just give you two more. You're a married woman, and a man at work begins to be very friendly with you. He invites you to meet him for coffee just to talk about business of course. You sense in your heart a bit of conviction that this is not wise, and when you do, you should immediately cut it off before it becomes a real problem. You have had an argument with someone in your family, and God is urging you to be the one to make peace. Do it quickly before you talk yourself out of it, and it will prevent you from sinning by staying angry. The Bible teaches us in Romans 13:14 to make no provision for the flesh, and part of what that means is not to make excuses for it or give it opportunity. The married woman who decides to have coffee with a coworker after having received conviction from God that it would be wrong is giving sin opportunity.

I once read a story about a little girl who was walking along a mountain path and it was very cold outside. A serpent slid up next to her and begged her to pick him up and let him rest inside her coat. For a while she resisted, but eventually gave in to his pleading. After a short while he suddenly bit her, and she cried out, "Why did you bite me after I was so nice to you?" The serpent replied, "You knew what I was when you picked me up." I think we can all relate to this short story. Surely we have all had times in our life when we have known deep down inside that we should not do a certain thing, but as temptation continued we gave in and did it, only to have bad circumstances as a result. We all make mistakes, but we don't have to continue making them. Learning from our mistakes is one of the wisest things we can do.

God instructs us to strip off and throw aside every weight and the sin that so easily besets us (Heb. 12:1). This gives the feeling that we must deal with sin harshly and quickly, and if we do, we will reap the reward of right living. We will also have peace in our heart knowing that we have done the right thing.

I am very grateful for forgiveness from sin, but I don't want to need it every time I turn around. It is my desire to discipline myself to make the right choices so I can have the joy of believing that I have pleased God.

Hidden Sin

We cannot deal harshly and effectively with sin if we make excuses for it or keep it hidden. We should all examine our hearts and be bold enough to be honest with ourselves about any sinful behavior in our lives. The apostle Paul said that he worked diligently to maintain a conscience that was void of offense toward God and man (Acts 24:16). WOW! He worked at detecting and keeping sin out of his life. Paul knew the power of having a clean conscience before God. We should make every effort not to sin, but when we do we should never make excuses for it, or keep it hidden. Our secrets can make us miserable, but the truth makes us free.

Whatever is not of faith is sin (Rom. 14:23). If we cannot do what we do in faith, then we should not do it. If a thing is sin then call it sin, don't call it your problem, your hang-up, or your addiction. Sin is ugly, and if we cloak it in better sounding words, we are more likely to keep it.

We should examine our life in the light of God's Word, and anything that does not agree with it should be seen for what it is and resisted with all our God-given ability. If we ask Him, God will always help us. We are partners with God, and He never expects us to do anything without His help. Let me say one more time: don't hide sin, get it out in the open, call it what it is, and don't make excuses for it or blame your bad choices on anyone else. Receive God's complete forgiveness for past sins and work with the Holy Spirit to aggressively resist all temptation in the future.

Now, do yourself a favor and forgive yourself totally and completely. Give up all anger you might have toward yourself for any perceived failures on your part, and start living the good life God has prearranged and made ready for you to live (Eph. 2:10).

Are You Angry at God?

If you have heard anything about God, you have heard that He is good and that He loves us. So naturally, we wonder why there is so much pain and tragedy in the world. If God has all power and can do anything He wants to, then why doesn't He prevent suffering? These questions and others like them have perplexed mankind as long as time has existed.

Children are abused, we constantly hear of wars and devastation, and world hunger claims millions of lives. The good sometimes die young, while wicked and seemingly useless people live to be old in age. Disease is rampant in the earth, and it attacks good people as well as evil ones. "It isn't fair!" our souls scream out. Where is justice? Where is God?

For the person who is looking for an excuse not to believe in God, they need go no further than these unanswered questions. They simply say, "If there really was a God, He would prevent suffering; therefore, I cannot believe He exists." But there are also those millions of beautiful people who do believe in God even though they have no answers to these perplexing questions.

If you are hoping I will give you a good answer

concerning these things, I want to say right now that I don't have one. I cannot sufficiently explain them, nor do I truly believe anyone else can. I have simply chosen to believe in God because to be honest, without Him, I don't think I would want to be alive. He is my life, and I would rather have a relationship with God and not understand everything about Him than try to do without Him.

God has never promised a life without suffering, but He has promised to comfort us and give us the strength to carry on. He has also promised to work good out of everything that happens to us if we love Him and continue wanting His will in our lives (Rom. 8:28). I am not happy when I have problems that cause suffering in my life, but I am glad that I have God to help me through them. I pity those who suffer without hope and whose minds and hearts are filled with bitterness because they cannot see beyond their pain.

We know that God is good but that evil also exists in the world. God has placed before us good and evil, blessing and cursing, and He has given us the responsibility of choosing one or the other (Deut. 30:19). Because many choose sin and evil, we have the effects of sin in the world. Even a good person still lives under the weight of existing in a sinful world. We feel the pressure of evil and long for the time when it is gone. The Bible tells us even creation groans under the bondage of decay, and it waits for freedom the same as mankind (Rom. 8:18–23).

We serve an invisible God who is a mystery! We can know Him in certain ways, but part of Him will always be beyond our understanding.

> Oh, the depth of the riches and wisdom and knowledge of God! How unfathomable (inscrutable, unsearchable) are His judgments (His decisions)! And how untraceable (mysterious, undiscoverable) are His ways (His methods, His paths)!
>
> *Romans 11:33*

We can know His character and put our trust in His faithfulness to always be with us, but we cannot understand everything God does, or does not do. Faith means that we believe in what we cannot see and often cannot understand. We have faith while we wait for the unveiling of these mysteries, and if we are honest, we realize that some of these answers may not come to us as long as we are here on this earth. God asks us to trust Him, and there is no need for trust if we have no unanswered questions. Before we can be content in life we must be comfortable "not knowing."

Intimacy Is Deepened by Suffering

One of the most mysterious and challenging statements in the Bible is Hebrews 5:8–9: "Although He was a Son, He learned... obedience through what He suffered and, (His completed experience) making him perfectly (equipped), He became the Author and Source of eternal salvation to all those who...obey Him." Jesus' sufferings were apparently the means of His perfecting (maturing), and it will not be otherwise with His disciples.

Faith cannot be matured without being tested. God gives us faith as a gift, but that faith only grows and increases as we use it.

The original twelve disciples had many things in their walk with Jesus that they did not understand, and Jesus told them, "You do not understand now what I am doing, but you will understand later on" (John 13:7). We live in a world of mystery and unexplained events, and God expects to be trusted.

J. Oswald Sanders said in *Enjoying Intimacy with God*, "If we are to experience serenity in this turbulent world, we will need to take firmer grasp on God's sovereignty and trust His love even when we cannot discern His purpose."

There are things that we learn in difficulty that

we cannot learn anywhere else. In Isaiah 45:3 the Lord said, "I will give you the treasures of darkness and hidden riches of secret places." There are treasures that can only be found in darkness. One of those treasures is intimacy with God.

Reasoning

Man in his natural state wants to understand everything. We want control and we don't like surprises. We would love it if all our plans came to pass in our desired timing, but they don't. If we do believe in God, then we ask Him to give us what we want, but He doesn't always do that. So, we end up with unanswered questions, and our nature fights against it.

Trying to figure out something that we are never going to get answers to is very frustrating and perplexing. After years of suffering mentally and emotionally trying to understand why bad things happen to good people, including why I endured over ten years of sexual abuse from my father, I came to a crossroads in my walk with God. I knew that I had to make a decision to trust God implicitly without having all the answers or I would never have any peace. I personally believe that is a personal decision that every person must make. If you are waiting for someone to explain God to you, then you will be waiting forever. God is beyond our understanding, but He is beautiful and amazing, and in the end He always brings justice to our lives. God trusts us with the unexplained!

Bad things do happen to good people, and it is their privilege to trust God.

> Who among you fears the Lord? Who obeys the voice of His Servant? Who walks in darkness and has no light? Let him trust in the name of the Lord and rely upon his God.
>
> *Isaiah 50:10 NKJV*

The tests we face in life can be shortened when we react to them in a mature manner, and we will emerge knowing God in a deeper way than ever before. I think most of us would say that the majority of our spiritual growth has been gained in times of difficulty rather than times of ease.

I turn to Psalm 37 quite frequently for comfort when I find myself in a perplexing situation. In the first eleven verses we are told that we are not to fret because of evildoers, because they will soon be cut down. We are to trust in the Lord and do good, and we will be fed by Him. I believe that means that He will supply us with what we need in life. Not necessarily all that we want, but surely He provides what we need.

Psalm 37:8 tells us that we are to cease from anger and forsake wrath because it tends only to evildoing. If we let the evil of other people keep us angry, we may end up doing evil ourselves. We also have a wonderful promise... "But the meek (in the end) shall inherit the earth and shall delight themselves in the abundance of peace" (Ps. 37:11). The meek are those who humble themselves and trust God no matter what their circumstances in life may be.

The apostle Paul said that he had determined to know nothing but Christ and Him crucified (1 Cor. 2:2). It seems that Paul perhaps also got weary of trying to find a good explanation for all things and decided to simply know Christ.

We are to trust in the Lord with all our mind and heart and lean not to our own understanding (Prov. 3:5). This proverb further tells us to be not wise in our own eyes (Prov. 3:7). To me this means that I am not to think for one moment that I am smart enough to run my own life or find the reasons why God does what He does. If I could ever understand God, then He could not be my God. God must be greater than we are in every way or He is not God at all. God is said to be without beginning and without end. We cannot understand that initial statement about God, so why would we understand everything else?

God does reveal certain things to us and He does give us answers to many things, but He does not give us answers to all things. We know in part according to His Word, but the time will come when we know even as we are now known.

> For now we are looking in a mirror that gives only a dim (blurred) reflection [of reality as in a riddle or enigma], but then [when perfection comes] we shall see in reality and face to face! Now I know in part (imperfectly) but then I shall know and understand fully and clearly, even in the same manner as I have been fully and clearly known and understood [by God].
>
> *1 Corinthians 13:12*

Why Didn't God Intervene?

It is difficult to understand why God doesn't intervene in our suffering when we know full well that He could easily do so. When James was in prison, he was beheaded, but when Peter was in prison, he was delivered by an angel and conducted to a prayer meeting. Why? The only answer is, "You don't know now what I am doing, but later you will understand."

Perhaps we are not capable of handling the knowledge we think we want. Maybe God withholds information from us in His mercy. I have decided that I will believe that God never does anything in my life, nor does He ask me to do anything, unless it will eventually work out for my good. This decision has brought much peace to me.

You may remember that earlier in the book I said that if we want peace, we must pursue it and go after it wholeheartedly. In my personal pursuit for peace, I discovered that peace and joy come through believing (Rom. 15:13), and that is what I decided to do. I don't do it perfectly, but God is helping me learn to respond to things I don't understand with "I trust You, Lord" rather than "I'm confused, Lord, and I need to understand what is happening." We can all make this same decision to respond with faith instead of doubt, and in fact the Holy Spirit is urging you to do so right now unless you already have.

I am not talking about believing in a general way, but believing in and trusting God in and through every situation in your life. It is quite easy to believe God *"for"* things, but He wants us to believe Him *"in"* things and *"through"* things.

Job

I suppose if I am going to include a chapter on unexplainable suffering I need to talk about Job. He was a righteous man who endured suffering beyond anything I have ever heard of. Job held tight to his faith for a long time, but eventually he began demanding answers from God. God spent four entire chapters answering Job, and in essence He said, "Job, if you are so smart, then why don't you try being God for a while. You run the world and see how you do." Of course in the end Job humbled himself and realized he was speaking foolishly. Then Job said an amazing thing and one that many of us are able to say after having endured terrible suffering:

I had heard of You [only] by the hearing of the ear, but now my [spiritual] eye sees you.

Job 42:5

In Job's trial, he came to know God in a way that he had never known Him previously. Prior to his suffering he had known about God, had heard of Him, but now he knew Him! I know of a young man who died of cancer, and although his suffering was terrible, he said, "I wouldn't trade this experience for anything, because in it I have come to know God in an intimate way." Does that mean that God arranges this kind of suffering just so we can get to know Him? No, I don't think so, but He does use it for our spiritual benefit.

Jesus

If we want to discuss unjust suffering, then we must talk about Jesus. Why didn't God come up with some other plan for the redemption of man other than allowing His own Son to suffer the horrors of crucifixion, and suffer the agony of taking all of man's sin upon His sinless self? Perhaps like any good father He is saying, "I won't ask you to go through anything I have not gone through Myself." As I said earlier, I don't have the answers to all these questions, but do we have to have them in order to believe in God? I think not! Faith goes beyond understanding, and in fact it often replaces it.

When I started this chapter I was searching my heart to see what God wanted me to give as an answer to those who are angry with God because of the suffering and disappointment in their lives. I realized within a few moments that He didn't want me to try to give one, because there is none we will understand. There are multitudes of books available that make an attempt to explain God, and some do a very good job, but I am not going to do that. I am simply saying that you can choose to not be angry, and if you make that choice, you will be doing yourself a favor because being angry with God is supremely foolish. He is the only one Who can help us, so why shut off our only source of help?

I know that if you have been hurt badly, part of you may be screaming right now, "Joyce, that is just not good enough." If you are, I understand, and I can only pray that soon you'll be weary enough of being miserable that you will say with Job, "Though He slay me, yet will I trust Him" (Job 13:15 NKJV).

Mad at God?

A woman I know whom we'll call Janine told me about a long period of time when she was angry with God. A Christian since childhood, Janine always looked forward to the time when she would meet a good Christian man, fall in love, marry, and raise a family. After college, she moved to New York City to pursue a teaching career. Janine found a good church and soon became an active member there, getting involved in the life of the congregation. She made good friends there, too, and was part of a large group of singles. After a couple of years, many of her friends from church got married and started families of their own.

Janine's twenties slid into her thirties, and all the while she continued to pray that God would provide her with a husband and family of her own. God blessed her career, and soon Janine was an assistant principal in the high school where she had taught. It seemed to her that God was blessing every part of her life except for the one that she cared about most. Her friends started having babies, and many of them moved away from New York in order to raise their children in places more family-friendly.

Janine continued to work hard and stayed active in church. But she just couldn't understand why God hadn't allowed her to have the single desire of her heart: a husband and family of her own. She started to get angry with God. Why was He so silent? After all, Janine wanted something that is good and natural; God says in Genesis that it isn't good for man to be alone. She began to pray for peace, reasoning that if God was going to say no to her prayer for a husband, then at least she wanted to feel a sense of contentment with the good things God had blessed her with.

But the years continued to pass, and Janine continued to be alone. While she enjoyed many things in her life, the loneliness she experienced became more and more of a thorn in her side. Why in the world wouldn't God honor her prayer and give her something as natural and wonderful as someone to love? She just couldn't understand why God would say "no" to such a simple prayer. The peace that she had prayed for didn't come, either. Why was God so silent?

One day Janine had an epiphany. As she was praying, begging God for some resolution in her feelings, she envisioned Jesus in the Garden of Gethsemane, asking God to take away the cup of death from Him as He anticipated His crucifixion. At the end of His prayer, He said, "Not my will, but thine." God said "no" to Jesus that day. It was necessary for Jesus to undergo the torture of the cross in order to save mankind.

Janine realized at that moment that if God could say no to His son and Jesus could take no for an answer, then Janine could take no for an answer, too. Nothing had changed, but everything changed for Janine. For the first time in over a decade, she realized that she didn't need to know all the answers—that God is God—and if she had to remain single for the rest of her life and never understand why, she could do it.

A couple of years later, when Janine was forty-three, she met a wonderful Christian man and married him two years later. Janine told me that if she had it to do over again, she wouldn't waste the time and emotion she had railing against God because He seemed silent. She would spend that time enjoying the blessings she had and doing her best to accept God's decision in the matter.

Sometimes God says "no" to things we want that are good and acceptable. Sometimes He says "not now." While we'll never know why in this life, we can use the time we have making the most of the life God has given us, or we can spend it agonizing in confusion and being miserable. Which do you think is the better use of time? For me, I prefer to use my time in a way that is productive—even if I don't know all the answers.

A Child Prays and Continues to Suffer

As a child being abused sexually, mentally, emotionally, and verbally by my father, I prayed often to God that He would get me out of the situation I was in, but He didn't. I prayed that my mother would leave my father and that she would protect me, but she didn't. In my childish lack of wisdom, I even prayed for my father to die, but he lived on and on and continued his abusive behavior.

Why? That question loomed large inside me for many years. Why didn't God rescue a little girl who cried out to Him? Even after I was a grown woman in ministry I still had the "why" question, and who wouldn't? God did show me that there are times when innocent people suffer in the path of the wicked. My father had authority over me as a parent, and he made choices that were evil and those choices affected me. Even with that I still knew that God could have put an end to the situation, but He chose to do something else instead. He gave me the courage and strength to go through it and overcome it. He has allowed me to use my pain to help other people and in so doing has actually worked it out for my good and the good of many others whom I have been able to empathize with and help. For many years I said, "If only I had not been abused, my life could have been better." Now I know better; I believe my life has been more powerful and fruitful because of it. One of the ways that God shows His awesome power is by helping ordinary people overcome horrible tragedies and then emerge with a good attitude and the experience to help someone else. I am grateful to say that I have had the privilege of being one of those people. I have to say, "Thank You, Lord, for giving me the best answer to my prayer, not just the one I wanted."

I can only pray that the things I have said about anger toward God will be of benefit to some of my readers. I haven't tried to give you an answer to unanswerable questions, but I have tried to honestly share my heart on the subject. Please trust God no matter what has happened to you or to anyone you know. No matter what happens in this world, God is good and He loves you! If you have been tormenting yourself with the question "Why, God, why?" I urge you to make a decision to cast all of your care onto God and say instead, "I trust You, Lord, no matter what!"

CHAPTER
7

Help Me: I'm Angry

If you're an angry person who is reading this book, first of all let me commend you for being willing to study in an area where you need help. I firmly believe that you can and will overcome out-of-balance, sinful anger. Some anger is sinful and some isn't, so I want to discuss them both just to make sure you have clear understanding.

Anger That Is Not Sin

God has given us the emotion of anger to let us know when we or someone else is being treated unjustly. This type of anger is referred to as *righteous anger*, and its purpose is to motivate us to take godly action to rectify the wrong.

When one of our daughters was about seven years old, she had trouble making friends in a new school she was going to. We lived close to the school, and one day I happened to drive by it on my way to run an errand. I noticed my daughter sitting by herself in the schoolyard, looking very lonely while all the other children were playing. I felt angry because she was being mistreated, and the anger I felt wasn't sin. I responded by praying for her and asking God to give her friends. If I had responded by going on the school property and yelling at the other children, my anger would have been wrong.

I think it is very important to understand that every time we feel angry it does not mean we are sinning. There are lots of things that stir up the emotion of anger, but how we manage that feeling is the most important thing.

There is such a thing as righteous anger, and in Psalm 78 we see that God became righteously angry against those who worshipped idols. How ridiculous to worship a stone statue when we can worship the living God of all creation. In God's righteousness He punished this kind of unrighteousness in the hopes that it would cause the people to repent and turn back to Him. This punishment was intended to help the people, not harm them. Righteous anger always takes action that is intended to help.

This is the same type of anger we have toward our children when they do things we know will harm them. We display our anger and correct them in order to help them.

When I visited Cambodia and saw children living in the city trash dump, picking through the garbage trying to find food to eat and pieces of glass or plastic to sell, I was grieved in my heart and felt righteously angry against that kind of injustice. I didn't just stay angry; I decided to do something about the injustice. Our ministry bought buses and equipped them as classrooms and a restaurant so we could feed and teach the children each day. The buses also have showers so the children can clean up and receive new clothes when needed. This was a good response to the anger we felt. God's Word tells us that the only way to overcome evil is with good (Rom. 12:21).

This kind of anger is not sin. It is actually good because it moves us to take action.

Many people today are angry about injustice, but they just stay angry and become angrier and angrier. They spend their time getting others angry by their negative talk and attitude, and no positive action is taken to correct anything. They often have an attitude of hopelessness. They decide that nothing will do any good, so they don't bother to try. This is a type of anger that easily turns into sin.

A mother's thirteen-year-old daughter was killed by a drunk driver who was given a very light sentence by a judge. The mother of this girl was very angry, but she decided to turn her anger into something positive, so she formed an organization called MADD (Mothers Against Drunk Driving). This organization has been instrumental in legislative reform for stricter laws against drunk drivers. She could have spent her life in anger and bitterness; instead she *overcame evil with good.*

I was very angry with my father for the abusive treatment he gave me. I hated him and seethed with anger for years, but I finally realized the only way to overcome the evil done to me was to do something good to help others. That is one of the reasons I have spent the past thirty-five years teaching God's Word and helping people who are hurting.

A man named William Wilberforce became so angry about slavery in England that he spent most of his life fighting against it and working for legislation to make it illegal. History is filled with people who became angry about injustice and fought to bring positive change. Sadly, history is also filled with people who became angry and then resentful and bitter and finally filled with hatred. They often took action that brought harm to multitudes of people.

Every era has witnessed some kind of injustice, and ours is no different, but anger that eventually turns to hatred is not the answer. Hatred is a strong emotion. We never hate someone a little. It is a demanding emotion. It demands the mistreatment of the one who is hated. Hate begins as anger. It uses up all your energy for living. It eats at you like a progressive disease and fills your thoughts and conversation. It makes you bitter, hateful, sour, and mean. It renders you unusable by God.

If you have already experienced injustice in life and have been hurt, don't keep the cycle going by hating.

The only answer to anger is forgiveness. Working through forgiveness is quite often a process. It begins with a decision to not only obey God, but to do ourselves a favor and forgive; however, the healing of our memories and emotions takes time. The second half of this book is dedicated to the importance of forgiveness and the "how to" of working through it.

Is Your Anger Valid or Distorted?

Before we can properly handle our anger, we must get honest enough to ask if it is valid or distorted.

The things people do that make us angry could be the result of something wrong in us instead of something they are doing wrong. Just because we get angry does not mean our anger is valid. In fact, probably a large percentage of people who are quick to get angry do it out of a wound in their soul they have never let heal. Angry people frequently become angry over things that we all deal with day in and day out without anger.

There were once things that Dave did that made me very angry, but those same things don't bother me now at all. He still does some of the same things, but I have changed. My anger was a result of my own insecurities.

If a person is insecure, they often respond to others in anger if they don't agree with everything they think, feel, and say. They perceive all disagreement as rejection, and the problem is really theirs, not the person they have gotten angry at. Insecure people need a lot of positive feedback in order to feel good about themselves, and when they don't get it, they often become angry.

Sometimes we simply get angry because we didn't get what we wanted when we wanted it in the manner in which we wanted it. The story that I'm about to share with you moves me deeply. It is a story of impatience and anger that cost a man a great deal—all because of anger.

A FATHER'S GIFT—Author Unknown

A young man was getting ready to graduate from college. For many months he admired a beautiful sports car in a dealer's showroom, and knowing his father could well afford it, he told him that was all he wanted for graduation. As the big day approached, the young man awaited signs that his father had purchased the car.

Finally, on the morning of his graduation, the boy's father called him into his private study. He told his son how proud he was to have such a fine young man and told him how much he loved him. He handed his son a beautiful gift-wrapped box.

Curious, but somewhat disappointed, the young man opened the box and found a lovely, leather-bound Bible with the young man's name embossed in gold. Angrily, he raised his voice to his father and said, "With all your money you gave me a Bible?" and stormed out of the house, leaving the Bible.

Many years passed and the young man was very successful in business. He had a beautiful home and wonderful family, but realized his father was very old and thought perhaps he should go see him. He hadn't seen him since that graduation day.

Before he could make arrangements, he received a telegram telling him that his father had passed away and had willed all of his possessions to his son. He needed to come home immediately and take care of things. When he arrived at his father's house, sudden sadness and regret filled his heart. He began to search his father's important papers and saw the still new Bible, just as he'd left it years earlier. With tears, he opened the Bible and began to turn the pages. His father had carefully underlined a verse, Matthew 7:11:

"And if ye, being evil, know how to give good things to your children, how much more shall your Heavenly father which is in heaven, give to those who ask him?"

As he read those words, a car key dropped from the back of the Bible. It had a tag with the dealer's name, the same dealer who had the sports car he had wanted. On the tag was the date of his graduation and the words: PAID IN FULL.

This story fills me with sadness. It is such a powerful example of the way so many of us lead our lives. Rather than accepting God's gifts with gratitude, even if we don't think they're exactly what we asked for, we get angry and cut off contact with

Him. Please don't do that! Remember that your Father loves you more than you can even imagine. He only wants good for you, even if he packages it differently than you'd hoped.

When we have a problem that manifests in abnormal anger, it is vital that we own the problem. We must take it as our problem and stop lashing out at others who really are not the problem at all. Many relationships are destroyed because of problems of this type. For a long time I tried to make Dave pay for what my father did by distrusting him and trying to control him so he could never hurt me. I actually had a bad attitude toward all men because one man had hurt me. I felt something was owed to me and was trying to collect from anyone in my life. Thank God I finally saw what I was doing and asked God to pay me back for the injustices in my life, and He did.

If you are angry let me ask you some questions. Is your anger doing you or anyone else any good? Is it solving the problem? Is it changing the person you are angry at? Is your anger increasing your joy and peace?

Do you believe you are a reasonably intelligent person? If so, then why would you keep doing something that is a total waste of time? Why not decide to do yourself a favor and let it go? Give the entire situation to God in prayer. Cast your care on Him and give Him the opportunity to care for you. Let God deal with the injustices in your life. In Isaiah 61 He promises to give us a double reward for our former trouble. I like that kind of payback, don't you?

You may be thinking, "Joyce, I can't make myself not feel angry." I agree, but what you can do is start praying for the people you are angry at in obedience to God, and that will help. The next thing to do is begin an intense study of God's Word on the subject of anger. God's Word has actual power in it that will enable you to do the right thing, and it brings healing to your soul. It is God's medicine for a wounded soul. Trust the Word of God. Approach it with expectation and faith. If you have a headache and you approach a bottle of pain reliever, you do so with an expectation that it will help relieve your pain. Approach God's Word the same way and take it as medicine for your wounded emotions.

The most important thing is to decide that you will not live an angry life. If you are firm in your decision, the problems you are having will get worked out. God will lead you in a particular way that will be just right for you. We always want a fix-it formula for all our trouble, but the truth is that we have to trust God and let Him lead us as individuals. The Bible is filled with wisdom that will help us avoid anger. Detecting and resisting anger early is the best plan. Don't let anger take root in your soul and become a problem that will be hard to deal with.

If you are an angry person, and have admitted it and are ready for help, you can get excited because you won't stay angry for long. You are on your way to an abundance of peace and new levels of joy. You will be able to love people in a godly way that will add power to your life.

A soft answer turns away wrath, but grievous words stir up anger.

Proverbs 15:1

When angry, do not sin; do not ever let your wrath (your exasperation, your fury or indignation) last until the sun goes down.

Leave no [such] room or foothold for the devil [give no opportunity to him].

Ephesians 4:26–27

Understand [this], my beloved brethren. Let every man be quick to hear [a ready listener], slow to speak, slow to take offense and to get angry. For man's anger does not promote the righteousness God [wishes and requires].

James 1:19–20

CHAPTER
8

Help Me: I'm in a Relationship with an Angry Person

We can learn to control our own anger, but we cannot control the anger of other people. We must learn how to handle the angry people in our lives in a way that will protect us and hopefully help them.

First, let's talk about anger that turns violent. I don't believe God has called us to be abused by angry people. My mother permitted my father to abuse her, and in the process, she ended up not protecting my brother and me. My father was verbally abusive to her, his language was often threatening, and his filthy cursing was a common sound in our house. He threatened to hit her often, and he did slap her in the face at times and even beat her. He was regularly unfaithful to her, and still she merely put up with it. She felt like she was being committed to her marriage, but in many ways I felt that she was disrespectful toward herself by allowing him to treat her the way he did. I realize she was afraid, but I wish with all my heart for her own sake, as well as mine and my brother's, that she could have either confronted him or left him.

Women from her era rarely got divorced; they just endured whatever kind of treatment they received. In our era people get too many divorces and often fail to make any effort to work through their difficulties. Both these extremes are wrong.

The data on battered women is staggering. According to the Bureau of Statistics, in the United States approximately 5.3 million women age eighteen or older are abused physically, verbally, or sexually each year. Every day, four women in this country die as a result of domestic violence. As I said, I don't believe any person should allow another to abuse them. It is not God's will for us to live in fear. Violent people usually make threats; they control with fear tactics. They are cowards who bully their way through life, and they need to be confronted for their own good.

I remember the fear that pervaded the very atmosphere of my home growing up as a child. I remember standing outside in the cold with my mom, waiting for my father to pass out when he was drunk in order not to receive beatings. I remember the screaming, yelling, cursing, threatening, pushing, shoving, hitting, choking, and beatings. I remember the rage, his fist held up to my face with threats of being hit. The fear I lived in became rooted in my soul, and it took many years of working with God before I was free from it.

If you are reading this book and you find yourself in an abusive situation, I implore you for your own sake and the sake of your children if you have any, please seek help. If you don't know what to do, get some counseling, call a hotline for battered women, or go to a shelter; but don't merely exist, waiting for the next time the angry person decides to take their anger out on you. People who abuse other people need help. They are sick people who don't know how to properly process their anger and frustrations. They have usually been hurt themselves and are reacting out of their own wounds. They need prayer for sure, but when we pray we must realize that we need to be ready to take whatever action God leads us to take.

The time came in my own life when I had to confront my father regarding the years he had abused me. I was approximately forty-five years old and was still suffering from what he had done to me. God showed me that confronting him was the only way to break the cycle of fear in my life. It was extremely hard for me to do because I knew I would experience his anger again and I did, but I also accomplished what God was leading me to do and it helped me break free. We must always do the part God leads us to do, no matter how the other party reacts.

Most of you reading this book are not dealing with the kind of angry people I have been talking about, but you do encounter angry people in your life, and some of you are in relationship with someone who is angry.

Because an angry man dictated my life for so many years, I was angry and vented my anger in both my words and my attitudes. My anger manifested frequently when everything did not go the way I wanted in life. I was wrong, and I needed godly confrontation as I mentioned earlier in the book. One of the best things Dave did for me was not allow my anger to make him unhappy. I believe one of the best things you can do for an angry person is to show them by example that there is a better way to live and behave.

Be an Example

Because I had never lived in an atmosphere where stability existed, I didn't know what it looked like. Dave was an example of stability to me, and that was extremely important. Had he merely told me to stop being angry and responded to my anger with anger of his own, I don't think I would have ever changed. As they say, "Two wrongs don't make a right." According to God's Word, we are not to confront anger with anger or evil with evil or insult with insult.

> Never return evil for evil or insult for insult (scolding, tongue-lashing, berating), but on the contrary blessing [praying for their welfare, happiness, and protection, and truly pitying and loving them]. For know that to this you have been called, that you may yourselves inherit a blessing [from God—that you may obtain a blessing as heirs, bringing welfare and happiness and protection].
>
> *1 Peter 3:9*

I am well aware that doing this is more difficult than reading about it, but anything God asks us to do, He will give us the strength to do if we are willing to be obedient to Him. God does have the solution to any problem that you have, and His ways always work if we will cooperate with them.

I believe with all my heart that Dave's example to me was what caused me to want to change. He was firm with me but never let me steal his joy. He let me know that if I wanted to be unhappy that was up to me, but he was going to be happy whether I was or not. He was consistent for a long period of time, and finally, I realized that I was missing a lot in life and I needed to change. Nobody can change until they want to, so if you try to change people in your life yourself it will only frustrate you. Only God changes people from the inside out, and He does it when we want Him to. So pray for angry people that they will let God work in their life, and be an example to them!

Are You Letting an Unhappy Person Make You Unhappy?

When I say in my conferences that we should not let someone else's attitude determine our level of joy, I always get an amazing response. I can see from the audience's faces that they have done that without even realizing they had another choice. Actually, we are easily controlled by other people's negative emotions until we learn that we have a say in the matter.

*   *   *

Marie had the opportunity to take a fabulous trip on the famous Orient Express train from Venice to Paris. She decided to invite her sister, Jean, on the trip as a fiftieth birthday present—all expenses paid. Jean accepted, and off they went on the trip of a lifetime. After a few days in Venice, Jean decided she missed her husband and children and grew unhappy. By the time she and Marie boarded the train for Paris, Jean was feeling angry. She just wanted to go home!

She also felt ill at ease in a country where she didn't speak the language and couldn't even get a cup of coffee without struggling to make herself understood.

Before long, Jean was angry with her sister. She felt that Marie was showing off because she could afford to take her poorer sister on a fancy trip. With each day, she started to resent Marie more and more, and her behavior became downright nasty.

Marie soon realized Jean was angry with her. Perhaps she was envious of Marie, who had traveled a lot and was at ease in new situations. Whatever the cause, Marie decided there were two possible outcomes: Jean could be angry, or Jean and Marie could be angry! Marie decided to be kind to her sister no matter what. She bit her tongue many times during the trip and decided she would enjoy this once-in-a-lifetime vacation even if Jean chose not to.

How frustrated Jean was when Marie chose not to respond to her anger! Marie looks back on that trip and is grateful she was able to savor each part of it, despite her sister's anger. Although she wishes Jean had had a better time on the vacation, she knows at least one person enjoyed it!

*   *   *

We are in for a sad life if we let other people determine our level of joy. Some people have already decided they are not going to be happy, and nothing we do will change their mind. I recently heard this statement, "A mother will never be any happier than her unhappiest child." That is actually usually true, but it doesn't have to be. We must realize that we don't help other people by being in a bad mood with them, and we can do ourselves a favor and keep our joy no matter what others do. The joy of the Lord is our strength, so keeping it helps us go through the situations we need to endure in life. Sadness weakens us, but joy strengthens us.

Can we really be joyful when other people we are around are angry and unhappy? Yes, we can if we set our mind to do so. And once again I want to stress that I believe it is the *best* thing we can do for the angry person. Just maintain a calm delight in their presence. Assure them that you love them and want them to be happy, but you are not going to let their decisions dictate your quality of life.

Don't become co-dependent on someone else's behavior.

I know how this works because not only did my father's anger control everyone else in the house, but I have encountered other situations like this in my life. I once had a boss who was frequently angry and often very difficult to please. I was happy when he was happy and upset when he was upset. That pattern had been established in my childhood, and I automatically responded to angry people by being afraid and intimidated. Thank God He has set me free, and He will do the same thing for you if you have a need in this area.

I also once had a neighbor and friend who was easily angered, especially if I was not doing everything she wanted me to do, and I responded to her the same way as I did my father and my boss. The devil will always make sure we have a supply of angry people in our lives if we allow them to control us, so we must have our mind set ahead of time regarding how we will respond to angry people.

If we encounter a person who is upset, naturally we should try to help them. But if they refuse to be helped, there is no logical reason for us to waste our time and energy. Getting entangled in other people's dysfunctional behavior is never wise. Do what you can do, but don't waste your life trying to fix someone who refuses to change.

There may be times when it will be best to disassociate yourself with the angry person. Of course, this isn't always possible if you are dealing with a family member, but we certainly don't need to keep angry friends.

In fact, the Bible teaches us not to associate with angry people:

> Make no friendships with a man given to anger, and with a wrathful man do not associate.
>
> *Proverbs 22:24*

Don't Blame Yourself

Whatever you do, don't receive the guilt and the blame that an angry person may try to put on you. Dysfunctional people almost always have a huge problem blaming all their bad behavior on something or someone. Blame relieves them of the responsibility to change. Don't take the blame! We must all take responsibility for our behavior, and even if you have made mistakes, that does not give another person the right to behave badly. If you have done something wrong, then apologize. But don't waste your days groveling in guilt.

The devil will work through any source he can to make us feel guilty and condemned. He knows that it weakens us and presses us down. Jesus came to forgive our sins and remove the guilt. He came to strengthen us and lift us up. Are you letting the devil steal your joy and strength through guilt? If you are, let this be the day you decide not to blame yourself any longer for other people's problems. Even if you did make mistakes in your dealing with other people, God can bring healing to everyone involved if they will let Him. The first step toward that healing is forgiveness and letting go of the past.

Pray—Pray—Pray

Don't just give up on angry people. Pray and continue to pray that they will see the truth and begin to walk in the light. They obviously have a bondage, a hurt, or something wrong in their past causing the anger. Let them know you are willing to help them but not willing to be their whipping post.

I remain amazed at the power of prayer, and the longer I live the more committed I am to praying as a first line of defense in every situation. I can recall making foolish statements like, "I've done all I know to do, there is nothing left to do but pray." Prayer should have been the *first* thing I did.

Remember Susanna? She went through a terrible time of suffering and desertion by her family and friends. Over the course of the past few years, she has learned to rely on the One Who will never leave us or desert us. She will tell you that she is now a different person than she was before her troubles began. She has learned to pray for those who hurt her. At first her prayers were halfhearted. She was angry with her ex-husband, her sister, and her children. As she prayed for healing for herself, she started to pray for healing for them. As often happens, as she put herself in their places, she began to realize that she had contributed to some of the damage she had sustained. She had used her wealth and power to control others around her. Now she is prayerfully working on letting others "be themselves" and not always trying to get her way. She is living a simpler life, and while she has many challenges, she says she is relying on God in a new, deeper way. Believe it or not, Susanna wouldn't go back to her old life even if she could. God allowed her to go through the fire, and while she has experienced much pain, she is also a much more compassionate person. Does she still suffer? Yes. But she will be the first to tell you that she now relies on

God instead of money and people, and her anger has melted.

I've seen amazing changes in people through the power of prayer. We cannot manipulate other people through our prayers, but through prayer we do give God an open door to work diligently in their lives, and He applies loving pressure on them in His own way. I cannot explain why sometimes we pray and get answers almost immediately, and at other times we pray for years and are still praying. But I am committed to keep praying and thanking God that He is working in the lives of the people I pray for, even if I am not yet seeing results. I believe when we pray God works!

> Keep on asking and it will be given you; keep on seeking and you will find; keep on knocking [reverently] and [the door] will be opened to you.
>
> *Matthew 7:7*

> The earnest (heartfelt, continued) prayer of a righteous man makes tremendous power available [dynamic in its working].
>
> *James 5:16b*

No one is ever beyond God's reach, and it is never too late for a person to change. If a hurting person doesn't know how to or is unwilling to go to God for help, then they need an intercessor. They need someone to stand in the gap between them and God and pray. Jesus fulfills this ministry for us, and we can and should do the same for other people. Never stop praying!

CHAPTER
9

Why Forgive?

Things couldn't have seemed more normal for the family of sixteen-year-old Brooks Douglass at dinnertime on October 15, 1979. While his mother prepared dinner for the family, his father, a Baptist minister, was studying for the sermon he would give the following Sunday at Putnam City Baptist Church in Okarche, Oklahoma. Brooks's younger sister, Leslie, was setting the table. A beautiful twelve-year-old, she was the reigning Miss Teen Oklahoma. Life was good for this young family.

When the dog started barking, Leslie walked outside and encountered a man who claimed he was looking for a neighbor the family had never heard of. When the man asked to use a phone, Brooks invited him in.

Within minutes, a second man burst through the door brandishing a double-barreled shotgun. The two men forced the family to the living room floor and hog-tied everyone except Leslie. They took her into the next room and proceeded to rape the young girl for more than three hours. The rest of the family could do nothing but listen to her agonized cries.

When the men were done, they went into the kitchen and ate the dinner that was still on the stove. For two more hours, they terrorized their victims and debated what to do with them next. Then they shot each one. Pastor and Mrs. Douglass, just forty-three and thirty-nine years old, died. The killers walked out with forty-three dollars and the couple's wedding rings.

The children suffered serious injuries and remained in the hospital, under police guard, for three weeks. But emotional healing would take far longer to arrive. For Brooks, the years following the shootings were a downward spiral. He enrolled in Oklahoma Baptist University but dropped out almost immediately. He bounced around from state to state, doing odd jobs and falling deeper and deeper into alcohol abuse and depression.

Later on, he made his way to Baylor University to

study for the ministry. But he had become a binge drinker and soon was suspended for low grades and a disruptive attitude. He finally completed college and went into real estate. He married, but his marriage failed.

In the ensuing years, Douglass slowly rebuilt his life, driven by the desire to bring his parents' killers to justice. He ultimately earned a law degree and ran for a seat in the Oklahoma State Senate, which he won.

In February 1995, while on a tour of the Oklahoma state penitentiary, Douglass came face to face with Glen Ake, one of the men who had killed his parents. He asked the warden if he could speak with the prisoner, who was on death row. Douglass had one question: *Why did you do it?* The two men spoke for more than an hour. Ake was extremely remorseful and cried throughout the conversation. As he got up to leave, Douglass told Ake, "I forgive you." When he said those words, "All of a sudden, it felt like it was poison pouring out of the bottom of my feet. It was one of the most physical sensations I've ever had, like someone took a clamp off my chest. I felt like I could breathe again for the first time in fifteen years."

Douglass went on to write and produce a film, *Heaven's Rain*, which tells the story of the tragedy and examines his journey from anger and devastation to forgiveness. He has said that the faith so carefully nurtured by his parents helped guide him to a sense of peace.

Brooks Douglass could well have continued to watch his life drain away in anger, pain, and resentment had it not been for his act of forgiveness.

Hopefully, if we understand the danger of bitterness, resentment, and unforgiveness, we will be motivated to do all we can to avoid it and it will help us be quick to forgive. We need to confront and press past these devastating emotions.

The feelings of anger are very strong and have a tendency to control our actions; therefore, the more we understand why we should forgive, the more likely we are to do so. Over the years I have learned many very good reasons why we should not stay angry and be quick to forgive that I will share with you.

Obedience to God

One of the first things that motivates me to forgive is that God tells us to. I don't think we always have to understand *why* God wants us to do something, but we should simply trust Him enough to do it. When we live in God's will, our lives are always much better than they would be if we followed our own will. I am sure you have seen the T-shirts that have "Just Do It" printed on them, and that is how we should respond to God's will.

Obedience to God is the best thing for us to pursue because it always adds peace, joy, and power to our lives. If we don't obey God we have guilty consciences, which always weaken us, and joy and peace are blocked. We may try to ignore the fact that we are disobeying and we may make excuses for it, but the effects of it still bother us. Nothing feels better than a clean conscience.

Are you mad at anybody right now? If so, why don't you simply obey God and forgive that person so you can get on with your life in peace, joy, and power? It has been said that Satan uses unforgiveness against people more than any other thing. He uses it to separate and divide, to weaken and destroy, and to hinder our fellowship with God. And these are only a few of the devastating effects of unforgiveness.

I believe that once you see how damaging unforgiveness is to your life, it will motivate you to do all you can to live free from it. I wasted a lot of years being angry and bitter; now my attitude is: "I've been there, done that, and have no interest in doing it again." I just told someone yesterday that I have no time to waste being mad at anyone.

*   *   *

Eva Kor is a real estate broker in Terre Haute, Indiana, vital and attractive at seventy-six years old. You'd never know that she suffered unthinkable torture at the hands of Dr. Josef Mengele as a child in the concentration camp of Auschwitz. In 1995, she returned to the camp on a mission, and that mission became a major news story throughout Europe. She read the following statement in the very place where she lost her innocence and her family: "I, Eva Mozes Kor, a twin who survived as a child of Josef Mengele's experiments at Auschwitz fifty years ago, hereby give amnesty to all Nazis who participated directly or indirectly in the murder of my family and millions of others."

Since then, Mrs. Kor has traveled the world speaking about her experiences at Auschwitz. Her message is always focused on the healing power of forgiveness. "Forgiveness is nothing more and nothing less than an act of self-healing—an act of self-empowerment. And I immediately felt a burden of pain was lifted from my shoulder—that I was no longer a victim of Auschwitz, that I was no longer a prisoner of my tragic past, that I was finally free," she says. "I call forgiveness the modern miracle medicine. You don't have to belong to an HMO. There is no co-pay; therefore, everybody can afford it. There are no side effects. And if you don't like the way you feel without the pain of the past, you can always go and take your pain back." Eva Kor is not wasting her time or her health. Obviously, her miracle medicine is God's prescription.

Let the Main Thing Be the Main Thing

Obedience is the main theme of the Word of God, and we need to let it be the main thing in our lives. Let us sincerely pray daily, "Your will be done on earth as it is in heaven." Our obedience should begin in our thoughts because those thoughts become our actions.

> [Inasmuch as we] refute arguments and theories and reasonings and every proud and lofty thing that sets itself up against the [true] knowledge of God; and we lead every thought and purpose away captive into the obedience of Christ (the Messiah, the Anointed One).
>
> *2 Corinthians 10:5*

The apostle Paul urges us to take our thoughts captive. Unforgiveness is birthed in how we think about people and situations. I have found that if I simply choose to believe the best of a person in a situation, then I can often avoid the agony of anger and bitterness. Or sometimes we can choose to just not think about an offense at all. One thing is for sure, the more we think about the wrong someone has done to us, the more angry and bitter we become, so let us make a decision to have our obedience to God begin in our thoughts.

The Amplified translation of the Bible says that forgiveness means to "drop it, and let it go." The way to do that is to refuse to think or talk about it. Get the offense off your mind and out of your mouth, and your wounded and stirred-up emotions will calm down.

They Let It Go

Men and women in the Bible who displayed God's power throughout their lives were always quick to forgive. Joseph is one of the best examples we find in Scripture and the apostle Paul is another. I mentioned Joseph earlier, but his story is so powerful and amazing that it is worth looking at it again and drawing more powerful examples from it.

Even though Joseph's brothers hated him and treated him cruelly, he was obedient to God when it came to forgiveness. He knew that vengeance was not his, but God's. He trusted God to work good things out of the evil situation, and that is exactly what happened. Even though Joseph found himself in many unfortunate and unfair circumstances, he experienced the blessings of God. God's favor rested upon him, just as it does on any of us who make obedience to God important in our lives. After many years of being a servant to other men and spending thirteen years in prison for something he was not guilty of, he still refused to have a bitter attitude. Eventually, God put him in a position of authority and power in the land, and during a time of famine, this is what he said to his starving brothers when they came to him for help:

Now therefore, do not be afraid. I will provide for and support you and your little ones. And he comforted them [imparting cheer, hope, strength] and spoke to their hearts [kindly].
Genesis 50:21

If we think about this for a moment, we will be amazed at Joseph's attitude, and we can all aspire to behave the same way when we find people to be mean and life to be unfair. Why should we forgive and be good to people when they have treated us badly? Because God said to do it! That is all the reason any of us should need.

Joseph's brothers lived in fear and agony during

their lives, while Joseph had peace, joy, and power. So I ask you, who was the victim and who was the victor? Initially, it might seem that Joseph was the victim; after all, his brothers sold him to slave traders. But in reality he gained a tremendous victory when he was able to go through that awful situation and come out of it a better man than he was before. His brothers ended up being the victims of their own hatred and jealousy. When Joseph made the decision to forgive, he did himself a favor that benefited him for the rest of his life.

The apostle Paul experienced many trials while trying to help people by preaching the Gospel to them. He found himself in jail and then on trial for crimes he did not commit. The Bible tells us that at his first trial everyone deserted him. Nobody stood by him, and that must have been a terribly lonely feeling and one that could have easily provoked bitterness. After all, he was on trial for trying to help the very people who deserted him!

> At my first trial no one acted in my defense
> [as my advocate] or took my part or [even]
> stood with me, but all forsook me. May it not
> be charged against them!
> But the Lord stood by me and strengthened
> me, so that through me the [Gospel] mes-
> sage might be fully proclaimed and all the

Gentiles might hear it. So I was delivered out of the jaws of the lion.

2 Timothy 4:16–17

Let me explore these two verses and share some things that I see. God stood by Paul and strengthened him, but that would not have been the case if Paul had been unforgiving and bitter. An unforgiving spirit separates us from God. Of course He never leaves us, but light cannot fellowship with dark, so we block or hinder the enjoyment of His presence in our life. However, Paul did experience the presence of God with him because he had been obedient. Paul also stated that he was delivered out of the jaws of the lion, and that was Satan working through evil people who accused Paul and sought to do him harm.

Quick obedience to forgive anyone we have anything against will give us power and authority over Satan. Let me remind you that Paul told people in one of his teachings to forgive to keep Satan from getting an advantage over them (2 Cor. 2:10–11). Does Satan perhaps have an advantage over you or anyone that you know due to unforgiveness? If so, you can correct it immediately by simply being obedient to God and forgiving completely anyone you have anything against. It is time to ask, "Are you holding a grudge or is the grudge holding you?"

The twelve disciples who traveled together had to forgive each other frequently for real or imagined offenses. When we spend a lot of time with the same people, they can get on our nerves and we imagine they are purposely doing things to irritate us. In reality they are just being themselves and we simply have had too much of them. I can imagine how difficult it must have been for the twelve disciples who rarely got away from one another for three years. They had opposing personalities and had to learn to get along just as we do in our experience with people.

Peter even asked Jesus how many times he had to forgive the same person for doing the same thing (Matt. 18:21). It is humorous if you use your imagination for a moment and think of Peter perhaps acting like an angry child being instructed by a loving parent in how to get along with his brothers. I can almost see Peter red-faced with anger, a pouting look on his face saying, "How many times do you expect me to forgive? Because I've just about had it!"

Would a disciple of Jesus think and behave that way? These twelve men were no different than we are. They were ordinary humans learning to obey God, and they had the same mental and emotional reactions that we do to the will of God. They felt rebellion, stubbornness, and all the fleshly resistance of any other person and they had to work with Jesus to overcome them. Don't despair if you have difficulty in the area of forgiving others. I don't know anyone who finds it to be easy, but we can do it with God's help.

The Ability to Love People

The ability to love people is hindered when we stay angry and refuse to forgive. I have written two entire books on the importance of loving people, so I obviously think it is something we need to give a great deal of attention to. Love is the greatest thing in the world; without it our lives have no flavor. They are dull, flat, and tasteless and we are locked in prisons of selfishness. God of course knew this before we did, and He has provided a way out of the horrors of such a life; that way is Jesus.

> And He died for all, so that all those who live might live no longer to and for themselves, but to and for Him Who died and was raised again for their sake.
>
> *2 Corinthians 5:15*

To me that is a beautiful Scripture. Jesus died so we can be free from the prison of self. When we are filled with unforgiveness we are filled with self.

We are thinking about what has been done to us, and what someone didn't do for us that they should have done for us. But what would happen if we thought more about what the person who hurt us is doing to him- or herself by disobeying God and mistreating us? Thinking about others always pays great dividends and frees us from selfishness. Jesus died so we don't have to live angry, bitter lives, and that is good news!

This may be hard to accept, but at its root, unforgiveness is selfish, because it is all about how *I* feel and what has been done to *me*. We may be hurting and have truly been treated unjustly, but turning inward and thinking only of ourselves do not help us recover from our pain. When God tells us to forgive our enemies quickly and show them mercy, it seems to be the most unfair thing in the world. But in reality He knows it is the only way for us to move past the pain and into the good life that is waiting for us.

I have found that I cannot be selfish and happy simultaneously, and I choose to be happy, so I have to forget about myself and keep reaching out to others.

The Bible teaches us to put on love (Col. 3:14). It actually says, "Above all that you put on, put on love." That phrase simply means that it is something we prepare for and do on purpose. I encourage you to plan every day to forgive anyone who might hurt you. Don't wait until it happens and then wrestle with the emotions of it, but instead set your mind and keep it set to live a life of Love.

*   *   *

Maggie married James when she was nineteen. Her goal in life had always been to be married and have a family. She was born to be a homemaker and couldn't wait to get started. Maggie had received a lot of affection in her family as she grew up, but James had received none and, sadly, he did not know how to give it. Maggie really missed and needed the outward display of affection. Although James truly loved Maggie, he did not give her hugs or kisses unless he wanted sex. He did not help with anything around the house or do much with the kids, because he never saw his father do it. James's mother waited on his father hand and foot while he sat in a chair; therefore, James expected the same thing from Maggie.

Because Maggie was so excited about being a good wife, she did everything for James and in the process reinforced his expectations for that kind of treatment. After twenty-five years of marriage and four children, Maggie got very tired of giving to her family while feeling she received very little in return. She rarely even heard words of encouragement or

appreciation from James, and even though she discussed it with him several times, he seemed unable
or unwilling to change. He thought she was being
emotional and told her so!

Maggie had been getting a little bit angrier as
each year went by. She was resentful, and a wall of
separation was erected between her and James. She
had a full-blown case of bitterness, resentment, and
unforgiveness, and became unhappier as time went
by. She finally came to a crisis point in her heart
when she knew that she either had to turn James
over to God and pray for him, or keep being miserable. She also started realizing that not only had she
let James take advantage of her, she had done the
same thing with her children. She did too much for
them, thinking she was being a good mother. What
she did in reality was give them an attitude of enti-
tlement that made them lazy and unappreciative.

She knew things had to change, so she decided
to start taking care of herself properly instead of
merely feeling sorry for herself. She continued to
take good care of her family, but she didn't do for
them what they could and should do for themselves. She actually sat down with her children and
explained to them that she had been out of balance
and things were going to change. She told them
what she expected and what the consequences
would be if they didn't do their part.

Maggie began doing some things that she enjoyed. When James or her family complained, she calmly and lovingly said, "It is right for me to have a life that I enjoy," and she simply did what she felt God gave her permission to do. Taking these steps of action helped her get over feeling bitter. She still wanted James to be more affectionate but realized only God could do the work in him that needed to be done. James was a good provider, and in many ways a good husband, so Maggie started focusing on the good points about him instead of the ones he lacked.

When she wanted James to do something in the house or with the kids, she just asked him to do it instead of getting angry because he didn't do it without her asking. Women want men to notice what needs to be done and offer to do it, but most of them declare that they are not mind readers and say, "If you want me to do something, why don't you just say so?"

These changes helped Maggie tremendously. Instead of having herself on her mind all the time thinking about what James wasn't doing for her, she prayed for him and tried to remember that he did not have a good example growing up. Her story is still in progress, but she is much, much happier now and James has given her a few compliments in the past couple of months. It appears that they are making progress and that is proof that God's ways do work.

Faith Is Blocked

Maggie had to let go of the unforgiveness in her heart before she could properly pray for James. Our faith won't work with a heart filled with unforgiveness. I wonder how many millions of people pray for others to change but their prayers go unanswered because they are trying to pray with anger in their hearts.

> And whenever you stand praying, if you have anything against anyone, forgive him and let it drop (leave it, let it go), in order that your Father Who is in heaven may also forgive you your [own] failings and shortcomings and let them drop.
> But if you do not forgive, neither will your Father in heaven forgive your failings and shortcomings.
>
> *Mark 11:25–26*

Faith works and is energized by love (Gal. 5:6). Faith has no energy flowing through it. It has no power where love is lacking. Oh, if only people would believe that and exchange their bitterness for mercy and forgiveness. Let us learn that when people do wrong, they truly hurt themselves more than they hurt us. May that truth fill our hearts with kindness and longsuffering toward people.

Here is a short recap of some of the devastating effects of unforgiveness:

When we refuse to forgive, we are in disobedience to God's Word.

We open a door for Satan to start all kinds of trouble in our lives.

We hinder the flow of love toward others.

Our faith is blocked and our prayers are hindered.

We are miserable and lose our joy.

Our attitudes are poisoned and we spew the poison onto everyone we meet.

The price we pay to hang on to our bitter feelings is definitely not worth it. Unforgiveness does have devastating effects, so do yourself a favor... forgive!

CHAPTER
10

I Want to Forgive, but I Don't Know How

It is easy to tell a person they need to forgive those who have hurt them, but what if they don't know how to? I have had the same people come to me over and over again, asking me to pray that they would be able to forgive their enemies. They were sincere, but unsuccessful. I have put together a process I believe we need to go through in order to experience victory in forgiving those who have hurt us.

Prayer is vital, but *we must do more than pray* in order to forgive. When we pray, God always does His part, but very often we fail to do our part; then we are confused about why it seems that our prayers were not answered. For example, a person in need of a job may pray for God to provide him with one, but he still needs to go out and apply at various companies in order to be successful. The same principle applies to forgiveness.

Desire

The first step toward forgiving our enemies must be a strong desire to do it. Desire motivates us to go through whatever we need to go through in order to reach our goal. A person who needs to lose fifty pounds won't succeed unless his desire is very strong. Why? Because he will need the desire to keep him going when he gets hungry or he has to continually say no to high-calorie foods while watching others eat them. I have a friend who recently lost sixty pounds. It took her close to a year of continual discipline to do it, and even now she must still discipline herself daily in order not to return to bad habits. What motivates her? She would like to eat more than she does almost every day, but her desire to be healthy and maintain a weight that is proper for her is stronger than her desire to eat.

I know we don't like to face this, but in reality we all do what we want to do if our desire to do it is strong enough. "I can't" usually means "I don't want to." None of us enjoys taking responsibility for the problem areas in our lives. We much prefer excuses and blame, but neither of them will set us free.

When people reach retirement age and they have saved enough money over the years to be financially secure, it's because they had a strong enough desire to motivate them to discipline themselves. They had to say "no" to some things they may have wanted in order to save for the future.

Strong desire will produce results in every area of our lives, and living free from bitterness, resentment, and unforgiveness is no exception. If you have no desire, then start by asking God to give you one because it is the foundation of all success.

I had no desire to forgive my father for abusing me until I started studying God's Word. Once I did, I saw the importance of forgiveness and that it was God's will for me to do it. I realized how much God had forgiven me for and that what He was asking me to do was no different from what He had done for me. The power in God's Word birthed in me a desire to be obedient in this area, and I believe it will do the same thing for you. If you have no desire to forgive your enemies, then study everything God's Word has to say about it, and I believe your heart will be changed. You will want to forgive, and once you want to, then the process can begin.

Decide

After you have a desire to forgive, then you must decide to do it. The decision cannot be an emotional one, but it must be what is commonly called a "quality decision." This type of decision doesn't change when feelings change. It is a firm decision that is determined to make forgiveness a lifestyle. This decision doesn't necessarily change the way you feel right away, and it doesn't mean that you will never struggle with the whole idea of forgiving people. Some people may need to be forgiven over and over and often for the same thing, and that is definitely not an easy thing to do. It is something that must be done on purpose without taking into account how we feel.

My father was a very harsh man in all of his mannerisms, and sadly I became a lot like him. He was the last person in the world I wanted to be like, but in some ways I was. My actions and tone of voice were often harsh, and I know that Dave had to forgive me over and over during the years God was working in me and softening my hard and broken heart. My healing took time and Dave had to be patient, but thankfully he didn't have to do it on his own. God gave him grace to bear with my weaknesses, and He will give you grace to deal with the people in your life also.

Sometimes I have to deal with people in my life now who behave the same way I once did, and I have to remind myself to do for them what Dave did for me. It isn't easy and I often don't feel like it, but I have made a quality decision to obey God and not live angry and bitter. Forgiveness is one of the most beautiful gifts that God offers us, and when we are willing to give it to others, it adds beauty, peace, joy, and power to our own lives.

God instructs us in His Word in the right way to live, but He will never force us to do what He says. He leaves the choice to each of us. There are many times in my life when I really wish I could make people I love do the right thing, but then I am reminded that God gives all of us free choice and He longs for us to choose the right thing so we can enjoy the life Jesus died for us to have.

Any time we obey God, we are doing ourselves a favor because everything He tells us to do is for our benefit. I remind myself of this quite often when what He is asking me to do is hard. Each of us must make our own choice; nobody can do it for us. I strongly urge you to make a quality decision to forgive. Once you have done that, then you will be ready to move on to the next step in forgiveness.

Depend

The next step in the process of forgiving others is to depend on the Holy Spirit to help you do what you have just made a quality decision to do. Just deciding isn't enough. It is vital but it is still not enough, because willpower alone won't work. We need divine strength from God's Spirit Who lives in us and is always available to help us do the will of God.

In God's Kingdom, independence is not an attractive trait, and it is not one that works. We encourage our children to grow up and become independent, but the more we grow up in God, or the more spiritually mature we become, the more dependent we are to become on Him. If we miss this point in our walk with God, we will always be frustrated. God does not bless what the Bible calls "works of the flesh," which is man trying to work apart from God. Even if we are working hard to try to do God's will, we still must depend on Him to make it successful. The Bible encourages us to acknowledge God in all our ways (Prov. 3:6). That means we should invite Him into all of our activities and tell Him that we know we won't be successful without His help.

Since we humans tend to be quite independent

and really like doing our own thing, this dependent attitude does not always come easy.

The Bible says in Zechariah 4:6 that we win our battles not by our might, nor by our power, but by the Spirit of God. God gives us grace, which is His power to do what needs to be done.

> I am the Vine; you are the branches. Whoever lives in Me and I in him bears much (abundant) fruit. However, apart from Me [cut off from vital union with Me] you can do nothing.
>
> *John 15:5*

I believe that John 15:5 is a pivotal verse in the Bible. Lots of other things depend on us understanding this single verse, which tells us that even if God calls me to do something or commands me to do something, I still cannot do it unless I depend on Him. He wants us to bear good fruit, to do good things, but we cannot unless we fully and completely rely on Him. Quickly forgiving those who offend us is good fruit and it pleases God, but we cannot do it unless we ask for His help and strength.

Are you frustrated because you're trying to do things that are just not working and yet you really believe they are godly things that you should be doing? Maybe your problem is a self-reliant and independent attitude. Why do we like to do things ourselves without any help? Simply because we like to get the credit and we like to feel proud of our accomplishments, but God wants us to praise Him for all of our victories and thank Him that He allowed us to merely be a vessel that He used.

We can want to do the right thing and still fail to do it time after time. The Bible says that our spirit is willing, but our flesh is weak (Matt. 26:41). It is important for us to learn that. It will help us to go to God in prayer at the beginning of every project and ask for His help. It will help us avoid wasted effort and frustrating failures. At our office we have recorded literally thousands of television shows, yet we never start one without gathering and asking God to help us. It took me years to learn that works of the flesh don't work; the only thing that does is dependence on God.

I well remember going to church and hearing a powerful sermon on something and being convicted in my spirit that I needed to change. Then I would go home and try to change and fail every time. This was very confusing for me until I finally realized that I was leaving God out of my plan. I had assumed that because what I was trying to do was His will, I would be successful. But I had to learn that nothing is successful if I don't depend on Him to make it work and give Him the glory for it when it does.

I believe that many people who truly love God are frustrated most of the time trying to be a "good Christian" because they don't understand this truth. I wasted years *"trying"* to be good, but failing to totally lean on God to enable me to do it. The Bible is filled with scriptures about the importance of depending on God and examples of people who failed because they didn't and those who succeeded because they did.

Isaiah told the people to stop putting their trust in weak, frail, and dying man whose breath is in his nostrils for such a short period of time (Isa. 2:22). God wanted the people to depend on Him so He could give them victory. His point through the prophet Isaiah was simply, why trust in man who is filled with weaknesses when you could trust God instead?

The prophet Jeremiah had a similar message for the people he ministered to. He said that we are cursed when we put our trust in frail man and turn aside from the Lord. But we are most blessed when we believe in, rely on, and trust in God, and put our hope and confidence in Him (Jer. 17:5,7).

The apostle Paul wrote to the Galatians asking

them if they thought after having begun their spiritual life with the Holy Spirit, did they now think they could reach perfection by dependence on the flesh (Gal. 3:3)? The obvious answer is no, they couldn't. Paul knew they would fail even at spiritual maturity if they didn't continue to depend on the Holy Spirit, and we will also fail at everything we try to do, including forgiving our enemies, if we don't depend on God for the strength to do it.

So we see that the first three steps in working through the process of forgiveness are desire, decide, and depend. Once you have done those three, you can move to the next one.

Praying for Your Enemies

God tells us to not only pray for our enemies, but to bless and not curse them. Wow! Seems rather unfair, don't you think? Who would want to pray that their enemies be blessed? Probably none of us would if we were following our feelings instead of the Word of God.

But I tell you, love your enemies and pray for those who persecute you to show that you are the children of your Father Who is in heaven; for He makes His sun rise on the wicked and on the good, and makes the rain fall upon the upright and the wrongdoers [alike].

Matthew 5:44–45

None of this means that we are to become a doormat for people to walk all over and that we never confront them about their bad behavior. Forgiving our enemies has to do with our heart attitude toward them and how we treat them. Jesus never mistreated anyone just because they mistreated Him. He confronted them in a spirit of gentleness and then continued to pray for and love them.

We are not to return evil for evil or insult for insult (1 Pet. 3:9). (Ouch!) Instead, we are to pray for their welfare, happiness, and protection, and truly pity and love them. I think this once again shows us that we should be more concerned for what our enemies are doing to themselves by evil deeds than what they are doing to us. Nobody can truly harm us if we obey God and put our trust in Him. They may hurt our feelings, but God is always ready to heal us.

Pray for people to receive revelation from God about their behavior because they may be deceived and not even be fully aware of what they are doing. Bless your enemies by speaking well of them. Cover their sin and don't repeat it or fall into gossiping about them.

I think the failure to pray for our enemies is one of the key factors in failing to work through the process of forgiveness. We start out intending to forgive, but if we skip this vital step that God has commanded us to do, we won't be successful. Like most of you, I have experienced some horrendous hurts at the hands of people I thought were my friends, and I admit that praying for them to be blessed was often done through gritted teeth, but I believe it is the right thing to do. Whoever forgives has power with God, and they are representing Him well.

Will you start praying for your enemies today? Will you practice this principle until it becomes your first and automatic response to offense? If you will, you will put a smile on God's face and yours as well. Anytime we obey God, we are doing ourselves a favor!

The last step in the process of forgiveness is to understand how your emotions respond to the whole idea of forgiving others. To put it simply, they go wild. Emotions definitely have a mind of their own, and if they are not controlled, they will control us. I have written a book titled *Living Beyond Your Feelings,* and I recommend that you read it for insight into understanding your emotions.

Our emotions are never going to completely go away, but we must learn to manage them. We must learn to do what is right even when we don't feel like doing it. I have learned by experience that even if I am angry with Dave, I can still talk to him and treat him nicely while I am working with God on the process of forgiving him. That discovery was a great find for me because I wasted a lot of years being angry for days and shutting him out of my life until my *feelings* were no longer hurt. I never knew how long that would take. Sometimes it was swift if Dave apologized to me quickly. But when he didn't apologize because he didn't think or even realize he had done anything wrong, it took days and sometimes weeks. Finally, when I had received my apology and felt better, I treated him better. That put my feelings in control instead of me, and that is not God's will for us.

It's one thing to be angry when a spouse commits a small offense and it makes us angry, but what about *big* offenses? Are there some that are just too heinous for forgiveness? Let me share two stories with you, and then you decide. Read them and think about how you would have responded in the situations.

Several years ago our chief media officer for Joyce Meyer Ministries, Ginger Stache, went through a very difficult time in her marriage. She and her husband, Tim, agreed to share their story in this book because they really want to help people who have been hurt. Ginger's heart is particularly tender toward women who have been deeply wounded in their marriages. Here is her story in her own words:

*　　*　　*

We were college sweethearts, married for fifteen years with two beautiful daughters. He was my best friend and life was good. So when I found out that my husband was addicted to pornography, my illusions of who he was and of our relationship shattered.

We weren't the happy, loving couple I thought we were. We were very active in our church; I was working in ministry, but was it all a facade? I was devastated, betrayed.

The emotions I felt were intense, swinging wildly from shock to disgust to grief. How could the man I shared my life with, the person I thought I knew best in world, do this? How could I have been so deceived? What else was a lie? But of the flood of emotions, it was anger that took root deepest.

I was furious with him for bringing this disgusting thing into our home and into our marriage. While some may disagree that he was unfaithful, for me there was never a question. When I thought his heart and passions were mine, they were somewhere else; he was focused on images of other women, fantasies of airbrushed perfection that did not really exist. How could I compete? How could I forgive him? Why should I try?

He was also in shambles. The dark thing he kept hidden for so long was now out in the light. He was ashamed, frightened, and somehow relieved. He promised to do whatever it took to get help, but I didn't care what he said. How could I ever trust him again? I was strong and definitely not the type to be fooled twice. I found the safest place to be was secure in my anger, to refuse to forgive; it would shelter me from getting hurt again.

And my anger was reasonable. You see there are two schools of thought where pornography is concerned. Some view it as harmless, victimless, nothing to get upset about. Others see it as too despicable to face, a problem for only the perverted, and much too vile for Christians to address.

When this ugly thing crashed into my life, I knew that both lines of thinking were wrong. *I* was a victim and I began to discover many other people I knew who were as well. Many of those Christians who thought they would never deal with such vile matters were silently suffering. I wasn't going to look away, and I certainly wasn't going to stay quiet.

I had decisions to make. Was our marriage going to survive this? Did I want it to? How would this affect our children? They were my greatest concern.

Realize it or not, you can't isolate anger to one person without it seeping out and poisoning the rest of your life. I couldn't allow my pain to affect my ability to be a good mother to my girls or keep me from God's call on my life.

Christ was always my place of refuge, and I had to be quiet in my rage long enough to allow Him to be that for me now. I sought Him in my pain, and His direction was clear. What He was asking of me was more important than my anger or my pride. It was the only answer. He was asking me to forgive.

I knew that I didn't have the ability in me, but forgiving Tim was the seed I must plant for healing to grow. It was a decision, not a feeling, and God promised to walk with me through it. God wasn't asking me to trust my husband; He was asking me to trust Him. How could I refuse my Lord who has forgiven me so much?

It was a daily choice and a very difficult one, but God is so very faithful even where we are not. He led us to a Christian counselor, an accountability group, and the seed of forgiveness I planted ever so slowly grew into fully blooming healing.

Now more than ten years later, we are college sweethearts, married over twenty-five years with two beautiful daughters who love God. He is my best friend, and life is good. Our love is far from perfect but stronger than ever. We work hard to communicate, trust in God, and forgive daily.

*   *   *

Jonas Beiler grew up like most Amish children, with a love for God and family, a good work ethic, and what many today call the trademark of the Amish community, an amazing grasp on the power of forgiveness.

Jonas left the Amish community to pursue his dream of owning a mechanics shop. As Jonas is often quoted as saying: "I loved horsepower rather than horses." He also married his lovely wife, Anne. Now you may know Anne better as "Auntie Anne," the world-renowned soft pretzel mogul.

Jonas and Anne lived a simple life on Anne's family farm, and they were as happy as ever. Jonas was a mechanic, and Anne was busy raising their two young daughters, Lawonna and Angie. As founding members of a thriving church, most of the couple's free time was spent working side by side with the pastor, who was also Jonas's best friend. The pastor relied heavily on the Beilers in their roles as youth pastors. But the contentment they felt during those days was about to vanish into a darkness so deep, so horrible, that by Anne and Jonas's own admission, it nearly claimed their lives.

Anne and Jonas were drifting apart; each of them suffering in silence as they mourned a tragic accident, the loss of their nineteen-month-old daughter, Angie. Anne had reached a place of total despair. Jonas's pastor had been praying with Anne one Sunday about the depression she felt over Angie's death. After the prayer he invited her to call him. Anne told Jonas what happened, and Jonas quickly agreed that it would be a good idea for her to meet with the pastor. After all, Jonas knew he wasn't able to help Anne, but maybe their friend could.

From the very beginning Anne could feel that something was not right about her meetings with the pastor. She chronicles one of the meetings in her book *Twist of Faith* as follows: "I couldn't believe how good it felt to talk about Angie, about the day she died, about how I felt... When the time came for me to leave... Pastor gave me another long hug, but this time when I looked up... he kissed me... Finally he pulled away and said, 'It's obvious to me, Anne, that you have needs in your life that cannot be met by Jonas. But I can meet them.' As I fled to my car, only one thing seemed certain in my mind: I could never tell Jonas... he would never believe me."

Keeping that secret would prove to be a grave mistake. With no one but the pastor speaking into

Anne's life, she was easy prey for his manipulation. Throughout the six-year affair Jonas never once questioned his best friend's loyalty, or that he had taken his wife for his own.

When Anne finally broke free from the relationship, she knew she would have to tell Jonas what had happened. Jonas says, "I stared at the wall after she left…I found my mind going into some dark places…my prayer was, 'Oh God, please don't let me see the dawning of another day.'"

The next day Jonas called a counselor who had been speaking at his church and told him what had happened. That phone call would set him on a path of forgiveness that would not only heal Jonas but also his entire family. The counselor told Jonas something that changed his life forever. He told him that "the only chance you have of saving your marriage is if you will love your wife the way Christ loves you."

For some people those words may have not been enough to calm the anger betrayal brings. But for Jonas it was enough. He attributes his ability to begin the forgiveness process to this: "Somehow, because of my deep faith and the rich tradition of faith in which I was raised, I reached deeper into my soul than ever before and found God giving me the grace to do things I never thought possible…it was the only hope I had: discovering how Christ loved me so that I could love my wife that same way."

God did bring Jonas to an understanding of His love. In return Jonas was able to show that love to Anne, forgiving her with the forgiveness Christ died to give us all. However, as Jonas will tell you, restoration of their marriage didn't happen overnight. He says, "Somewhere in all the pain, confusion and discouragement, I made a commitment ... no matter how I felt, I was going to do my best to continue ... It sounds like a great story today because it has a happy ending. But ... the insecurities still crop up from time to time. Recovering from something like this doesn't mean you'll have a pain-free marriage. But restoration is possible. Whenever I am given the chance to introduce my wife, I like to introduce her as ... my best friend, my wife, the mother of all my children, and the grandmother of all my grandchildren. It has always been my dream, when we were going through those dark times, that I would be able to say that.

"My dream came true because of Christ's love."

*   *   *

The individuals in both of the stories above were faced with devastating situations that triggered understandable heartbreak and hurt. They could

have given up and walked away from their marriages, but thankfully, by the grace and mercy of
God, they were willing and able to forgive. Yes, it
is amazing, but then, we do serve an amazing God!
We can thank God that He has given us the tools to
overcome our understandable emotional responses
to the type of pain we have just read about. Truly,
all things are possible with God.

If we are controlled by our emotions, Satan has
control over us. All he needs to do is give us a bad
feeling, and we behave accordingly. Surely you can
see that this will never do. We absolutely must learn
to live beyond our feelings. We can forgive those
who hurt us if we are willing to do so. We can pray
for our enemies whether we feel like it or not. We
can talk to people or refrain from talking unkindly
about them. We can do the will of God no matter
how we feel.

Our emotions are a part of our soul, and they
can be good and produce good feelings, but they
can also do just the opposite. They can serve God
or Satan, and we must make the choice which one
it will be. When someone hurts my feelings and
I let those wounded feelings control my behavior,
then I am playing right into Satan's hands. But if I
do what God commands no matter how I feel, then
I am exercising authority not only over my feelings
but over Satan, too. I have found a great sense of

power and satisfaction in being quick to forgive and praying for people who have hurt me. I know it is the right thing to do no matter how I might feel, and doing right always gives us spiritual satisfaction deep inside.

Your feelings are not the real you. Your will energized by God's will is the "big boss" in your decisions, even when emotions move and fluctuate. When they sink, we can remain stable. If we decide to do the right thing no matter how we feel, our feelings do eventually catch up with our decision. In other words, we can't wait to feel right to do right; we do right and then feelings come later. They may still fluctuate, but emotions do improve as we persist in being obedient to God's will. While you are doing what God has asked you to do, you can trust Him to heal your wounded feelings.

A good plan is to not consult your feelings at all when you are making a decision. Be led by the Spirit of God and His wisdom and never merely by how you feel.

We can't control what other people do and how they decide to treat us, but we can control our response to them. Don't let other people's behavior control you. Don't let them steal your joy; remember that your anger won't change them, but prayer can.

How to Pray for Your Enemies

There's no denying that it's difficult to even think about praying for someone who has hurt you, whether it's a friend, a stranger, or a loved one. But it can be done. Not only that, but I can assure you that like most things, it gets easier with practice.

*   *   *

Therese was a hard worker who had spent decades in the field of finance. When she was in her early forties, she was recruited by the top company in the industry for a high-level job that offered terrific pay and great benefits. She had been with her company for twenty years and was well respected by her employers and colleagues. Even in a shaky economy, she was quite certain that her current job was extremely secure. Did she really want to risk that to take a new job where she'd be the "new kid on the block"?

The CEO of the company that was offering her the new job, Steve, was a man she had worked for years earlier. She knew he was a good boss and a fair man. He assured her that he would make sure she was always treated fairly. After much prayer and consideration, Therese and her husband decided that she should accept the offer.

The new job was wonderful. Her responsibilities fit her talents well, and she thrived in the new company. There was one colleague who wasn't very nice to her, but that woman, Jackie, wasn't nice to anybody. Her personnel file was full of complaints from coworkers and subordinates whom she had treated badly, and everyone knew that she was trouble, including the boss. Therese did her best to get along with Jackie and didn't worry.

As time went on, Jackie's behavior toward Therese became meaner and more insolent, and Therese began to suspect that Jackie didn't want her at the company. One day at a corporate meeting, Jackie humiliated Therese in front of a roomful of vice presidents and lied about a big account that had been lost, blaming the whole fiasco on Therese.

Two days later, Therese's boss called her into his office and fired her. Jackie had told him the same lie, and he had accepted her word without even allowing Therese to speak in her own defense. Therese wasn't sure who she was angrier with, Jackie or Steve. At the age of fifty-one, Therese was out of a job, and the industry wasn't hiring.

Therese went home that night devastated. When it was time to go to sleep, her husband prayed out loud and then waited for her to do the same, a practice they repeated every night. As she prayed, Therese knew that she should pray for Jackie and

Steve. She also knew that she hated them at that moment. As far as she was concerned, both of them had betrayed her. Now she was unemployed, their lives were going on as usual, and she was supposed to pray for *them?*

"Lord," she prayed, "I know I'm supposed to pray for my enemies. That would be Jackie and Steve, who have put our future in danger for no good reason. I'm very angry with them, and I confess to You that I don't want to pray for them. But I have to. Please convict them about what they've done to me. In Jesus' name, Amen."

Therese told me that it took a couple of months, but each night she prayed for Jackie and Steve, and her prayers began to change. Before too long, she started praying for healing for Jackie's asthma, which was very severe. Then she found herself praying that Jackie's attitude toward her colleagues and employees would soften; that she would be kinder. Therese prayed that Steve would find a good replacement for her and that the people who had worked for her would like their new boss. She prayed for some of his personal problems that were common knowledge.

Little by little, Therese's feelings toward Jackie and Steve started changing. She told me that even though the hurt that she suffered at their hands did remain, it stung less as time went by, and she actually found herself praying that God would bless them—and meaning it! When Jackie was fired a couple of years later, Therese was actually very sorry for Jackie and reached out to her. No one was more surprised by Therese's kindness than Therese herself. But God had worked in her, slowly but surely.

So, how do you pray for your enemies? Just do it. You aren't going to feel like it at the beginning. But like Therese, you will experience healing in your own soul if you will obey God rather than obeying your feelings.

CHAPTER
11

Finding Hidden Unforgiveness

I recall going to church one Tuesday evening about twenty-five years ago and hearing the pastor announce that he would be teaching on our need to forgive those who had offended us. I smugly thought, "I have no unforgiveness at all." I settled in to hear a sermon that I was sure I didn't really need. But as the evening went on, I realized I did have unforgiveness in my heart, but it had been hidden. Perhaps a more accurate way of describing it would be to say I was hiding from it. We rarely find it comfortable to face our sin and call it what it is. We can stuff things so far down inside of us that although they are affecting us adversely, we don't even realize they are present. We often think more highly of ourselves than we ought to, and we can even judge another for their failures yet refuse to see our sin.

God revealed two specific situations in my life that night and clearly showed me that I did have an unforgiving attitude.

In the Bible we are told a story of two brothers who were both lost. One was lost in his sin, and the other was lost in his religion. They were each alienated from God in a different way. We commonly call this story the account of the Prodigal Son, and the focus is usually on the younger son who demanded his inheritance and promptly left home to waste his father's money on a sinful lifestyle. As most sinners do, he ended up in a huge mess. His money was gone; he was working for a pig farmer and eating the same food the pigs ate. Taking an inventory of his sad state, he decided to return to his father and beg for forgiveness and the favor of just being a servant in his house (Luke 15:11–21).

The father, who represents God in this story, rejoiced at his son's return and made preparation for a huge celebration in his honor. However, the older son was very unhappy and determined that he would not join the party. He felt that he had lived a morally righteous life, and he reminded his father of all the good work he had done and how the father had never given him a party. We can readily see that the religiously righteous brother was not happy about his younger brother's return and was in fact resentful and angry. He was lost in his own self-righteousness. He was proud of his so-called good works and determined that his brother did not deserve the good treatment he was getting. The older brother failed to realize that his attitude was even worse than his younger brother's bad behavior.

If someone had walked up to him and said, "You have unforgiveness in your heart," he would not have believed it. He was blinded to his sin by what he thought was morally righteous behavior. He had in fact been a good boy and followed all the rules, but God was not pleased because his heart was not right. If he had taken time to examine his attitude, he would have realized that he too needed forgiveness.

Six Attitudes That Reveal Unforgiveness

Unforgiveness Always Keeps Score
Reciting a list of his righteous behavior to his father, the elder brother said, "These many years I have served you." He had counted his good works and knew exactly how many years of good behavior he had to his credit. He had kept score, and we have the same tendency. We like to keep a record

of our admirable behavior and a record of the sins of others. We compare, and in our thinking we put ourselves in a class above others. Jesus came to destroy class distinction. If we sin, our help is in Him alone, and if we do good, it is only because He has enabled us to do so. He gets all the credit for any good thing we ever do. We are nothing without Him, and whatever we are is in Him, so all class distinction is destroyed and we are all one in Christ.

The elder brother counted his good works and his younger brother's sins. This is always a sign that unforgiveness is present in our heart. Peter asked Jesus how many times he had to forgive his brother (Matt. 18:21–22). He was obviously keeping a record of offenses. Love takes no account of the evil done to it (1 Cor. 13:5). If we are going to obey Jesus and walk in the kind of love that He shows us, we must not keep records of offenses. When we forgive, we must forgive completely, and that means that we let it go and remember it no more. We could remember if we tried to, but we don't have to. We can forgive, walk away from it, and not think or talk about it any longer.

There was a time when I could have recounted everything that Dave had ever done to anger me. I knew all his faults, and—believe it or not—I was haughty enough to pray regularly for him to change. Yes, I prayed for him and remained blind to my own bad attitude! Now I couldn't even tell you the last thing Dave did that angered or frustrated me. I did myself a favor and stopped keeping a record of all his faults. Now I am happier, and the devil is unhappy because he lost a stronghold in my life.

Ask yourself right now if you are keeping an account of what others do to you and what you do for them. If you are, then you are headed for trouble in your relationship and you do have unforgiveness in your heart that needs to be repented of.

Unforgiveness Boasts of Its Good Behavior
The elder brother told his father that he had never disobeyed his father's commands...he was boasting of good behavior while elaborating on his brother's sins. Judgment always says, "You're bad and I am good." The Bible is filled with lessons about the dangers of critical judgment toward other people. We reap what we sow, and the way we judge is the way we will be judged. If we sow mercy, we will reap mercy, but if we sow judgment, we will reap judgment (Matt. 5:7, 7:1–2).

The elder brother had no mercy, which is usually the case with self-righteous people. Jesus had some shockingly honest things to say to the religious Pharisees of His day. He said they preached what was right to do, but they didn't practice it.

They did all their works to be seen of men. They were pretenders (hypocrites) because they followed all the law but wouldn't lift a finger to help anyone. They cleaned the outside of the cup, while the inside remained dirty. In other words, their behavior may have been good, but their hearts were evil (Matt. 23). Religiously self-righteous people can be some of the meanest people in the world. Jesus did not die for us so we could have a religion, but in order that we might have an intimate relationship with God through Him. Real relationship with God softens our hearts and makes us tender and merciful toward others.

The night I sat in church thinking I had no unforgiveness in my heart, I could have told you exactly how many hours each week that I prayed and how many chapters of the Bible that I read. Yet I was unaware of a heart attitude that God disapproves of. I was the embodiment of the elder brother. Thankfully God has changed me, but I always take time to examine my heart and make sure I am not taking credit for the good that God does through me. The Bible says that when we do good things, we should not let our left hand know what our right hand is doing. That means we don't need to be thinking about it. We let God use us for His glory and go on to the next thing He has for us.

Do you compare how good you think you are to

how bad other people are? Do you make statements like, "I can't believe they did that. I would never do that"? If so, then you are headed for trouble. The more highly you think of yourself, the more lowly you will think of others. True humility doesn't think about itself at all ... it isn't self-focused.

If we think we are better than others we will always find it difficult to forgive them, so let us humble ourselves before God and erase all mental records we have of our own good works.

Unforgiveness Complains
The elder brother said to his father, "You never gave me [so much as] a [little] kid, that I might revel and feast and be happy and make merry with my friends" (Luke 15:29).

He had a martyr syndrome—"I did all the work, while everyone else played and had a good time." He was probably a workaholic, who did not know how to have fun and enjoy his life; therefore, he was jealous of anyone who did. He complained and complained and complained about the way he was being treated.

The night I sat in church listening to the sermon on unforgiveness that I thought I didn't need, God revealed that I had unforgiveness toward my oldest son because he wasn't as spiritual as I wanted him to be.

If you find yourself complaining frequently about a specific individual, there is a good possibility that you have some unforgiveness toward him in your heart. It may be some specific thing or things this person has done to you, or it could just be that his or her personality irritates you. In the case of my son, I was angry about his choices and yet failed to remember that at his age, my choices were even worse than his.

Forgive people you are angry at, find something positive to meditate on and talk about, pray and watch God work in you and in the people you love.

Unforgiveness Alienates, Divides, and Separates

The elder brother referred to his brother as "this son of yours." He would not call him "my brother" because he had erected a wall of separation in his heart toward him. He withdrew and refused to go to the party and celebrate with others. He separated himself not only from his brother but also from anyone who was rejoicing with his brother.

Have you ever been angry with someone and then gotten angry with someone else who wasn't angry with that person too? There have been times when I've complained to Dave about the unkind way someone has treated me only to have him start defending the person. He'd remind me they may have been having a bad day, and then he would talk about their good points.

He was trying to help me see more than one side of the situation. But I've gotten angry with him because he was defending the person I was angry with. My anger not only divided me from the one I was angry with, but it divided me from anyone who liked them. I think people who are offended and filled with bitterness live lonely, separated lives in most cases. They are so busy with their resentment that they have no time for anything else.

The elder brother was not about to come to a party. If he did he might enjoy himself, and he preferred to complain and be miserable. The whole subject of the tragedy of disunity is very important, and I will include more about it in a later chapter.

Unforgiveness Continues to Bring up the Offense
When we are unforgiving we keep finding excuses to talk about what people have done to us. We bring it up in conversation as often as we can. We tell anyone who will listen. These behaviors should be a sign to us that we are in disobedience to God and that we need to seek His help right away in letting the offense go. What is in the heart does come out of the mouth. We can learn a lot about our true selves by listening to ourselves.

The elder brother reminded the father that he was being good to a son who did not deserve it and talked about all of his sin (Luke 15:30). He was angry and his conversation proved it. Jesus said that when we are angry we are to let it go, and that means to stop bringing it up. Have you ever thought you had forgiven someone for an offense but discovered that the next time they did anything to irritate you that you quickly brought up the old offense? We have all done that. It means that we have not completely forgiven and we need to ask God for help.

Unforgiveness Resents the Blessings Enjoyed by the Offender

The elder brother was jealous and angry, and he resented his father blessing his younger brother. He did not want the prodigal brother to have a party, the fatted calf, a new robe, sandals, and a beautiful ring. He deeply resented it.

Resentment over other people's blessings reveals a lot about our own character. God wants us to rejoice with those who rejoice and weep with those who weep. He wants us to trust Him to do what is right for each person. The younger brother in our story had done wrong, but right now he needed forgiveness, acceptance, and healing. His father may have intended to speak with him about his wrong behavior later, but right now he needed love. He needed to see a display of the father's goodness and mercy. God always does what is right for everyone, and He has His own reasons for why He does what He does, the way He does it. Just because we don't agree or think it is fair makes no difference. If we keep a resentful attitude we will be the one who suffers for it.

Everyone else went to the party the father gave for the younger brother; only the sour elder brother refused to enjoy himself. His bad attitude would not let him enjoy the party. He really needed to do himself a favor and forgive.

Just to make sure you don't have any hidden unforgiveness, go over the list of things I have just mentioned and do it with an open heart. Ask God to reveal any bitterness, resentment, unforgiveness, or offense that you might have. Check for the symptoms of unforgiveness, and if you have any, then run to Doctor Jesus for healing.

CHAPTER
12

The Power and Blessing of Unity

Unity, agreement, and harmony are encouraged and commanded throughout the Word of God. The only way that can be maintained is if we are willing to be quick to forgive and generous in mercy. The world today is filled with disagreement. We regularly hear of wars, hatred, and upheaval in governments, church denominations, and business organizations of all kinds. Yet in the midst of all this, God offers us peace. We can choose which way we want to live.

Behold, how good and how pleasant it is for brethren to dwell together in unity!

Psalms 133:1

The psalmist goes on to say that where there is unity, the Lord commands blessing and life forevermore. God honors those who make an effort to live in harmony. Jesus said that those who are makers and maintainers of peace are sons of God. That means they are spiritually mature. They live beyond their feelings and are willing to humble themselves under the mighty hand of God and obey Him. They take the initiative and are aggressive in maintaining unity.

Think about the atmosphere you live or work in. Is it peaceful? Do people get along? If not, what are you doing about it? You can pray; you can encourage others to get along. And, if any of the lack of harmony is your fault, then you can change. You can stop arguing about things that really don't matter anyway. You can be the first to apologize when you have a disagreement with another person. One of the first good fruits that wisdom produces is peace. Walk in wisdom and your life will be blessed.

But the wisdom from above is first of all pure (undefiled); then it is peace-loving, courteous (considerate, gentle). [It is willing to] yield to reason, full of compassion and good fruits.

James 3:17

Choosing Unity

As I mentioned, there is turmoil everywhere we turn, so if we want unity and the peace it produces, then we must choose it on purpose. We must learn God's ways and work with His Holy Spirit in promoting peace.

Anyone who is married knows that more often than not, we find an abundance of things to disagree about. Usually we marry someone who is the opposite of us in personality, and that means that we don't think alike. We may disagree, but we can learn to disagree respectfully and agreeably.

Dave and I are very different, and we wasted a lot of years arguing until we learned the dangers of strife and the power of unity. We made a commitment to have peace in our relationship, home, and ministry. We firmly believed that God could not bless us the way He desired as long as we were divided. You have probably heard the phrase, "United we stand, divided we fall," and it is true. The Bible says that one can put one thousand to flight and two can put ten thousand to flight. We see from this Scripture how power is multiplied when we choose to live in agreement.

I was the source of most of our arguments. Dave

has always been a peaceful person, and he despises the stress that is created when we argue and remain angry. I was raised in a house where there was no unity, and I had to learn what peace was. I studied the Word of God and sought to learn what I needed to change in order to have peace. I discovered that there is no peace without humility. Humility is the chief virtue to be sought after and probably the most difficult one to attain and maintain.

A truly humble person will avoid all empty (vain, useless, idle) talk, for it will lead us into more and more ungodliness. They shut their mind against ridiculous controversies over ignorant questions, for they know that they foster and breed strife.

Can you remember the last time you had an argument with someone over something that was extremely petty and actually ridiculous? Perhaps you were having a bad day and said something that should have been left unsaid, and it started an argument. You could have quickly apologized, but your pride made you continue the silly conversation, trying to prove you were right. You wasted your day, were stressed out, got a headache, a knot in your stomach, and had no desire to pray. In your heart you knew that you had behaved badly, and a part of you wanted to say, "I am really sorry; this was my fault and I ask you to forgive me." But another part, your flesh, made you stubbornly refuse to do so.

I certainly remember many times like that, but thankfully I don't live that way anymore. I hate strife, turmoil, disharmony, and disagreement. Being right is not all it appears to be. We often strive with others just for the single purpose of proving we are right in a disagreement, but even if we do, have we really gained anything other than a smug, prideful feeling? I think we would be much better off if we humbled ourselves and let God be our vindicator. He is well able to prove us right in a situation if that is His best plan. God's Word states that love does not insist on its own rights (1 Cor. 13:5). It doesn't even insist on its right to be right! Are you willing to let someone else think they are right even if you don't believe they are, rather than start an argument about it? If you are, then you are one step closer to being a peacemaker and maintaining unity.

I was recently on a trip with about eleven of my family members that included Dave, two of our children, their spouses, and several grandchildren, some of them teenagers. We were all staying in the same house and had opportunity for disunity and hurt feelings. Not everyone wanted to do the same thing, or watch the same thing on television, play the same game, or eat at the same place. Teenagers can often have attitudes that are very frustrating, and then we have to remember that as teenagers, we didn't behave any better than they do now.

My point is that even though all of us on that trip are Christians who attempt to obey God and live in peace, we had to work at it, just as you will if your desire is unity. It is impossible to maintain a peaceful atmosphere in the situation that I have described unless everyone is willing to humble themselves and be generous in mercy and forgiveness. God well knew what He was doing when He instructed us in His Word to be quick to forgive. Satan is always lurking around trying to stir up trouble, but God has given us ways to defeat him. Be generous in mercy, be long-suffering and patient, be understanding, recognize your own sins, and it will help you not be quick to judge others and forgive quickly and completely so you don't fall into Satan's trap of strife.

Relationships are very important to all of us. Bad ones are tormenting, but good relationships are among the most beneficial and blessed things in the world. Satan seeks to destroy relationships because he knows the power of unity. He uses the differences in our personalities against us. He causes us to take things out of context that are said to us, he promotes hurt feelings, anger, and a rebellious attitude that refuses to forgive. But we do have authority over Satan, and we can resist him and all of his tactics to bring division into our relationships at home, work, school, church, or anywhere we are.

Ask yourself what the benefit of turmoil is. Does it do any good or change the situation? Most of the time strife just makes us miserable and does no good at all. Let's make a decision to work for and make peace. No one of us can solve all the turmoil in the world, but we can each be responsible for our own lives and relationships. Start praying and ask God what you might change to promote more peace in your life.

Be Adaptable

Most of us want our own way in things, but in order to have unity we must learn to be adjustable and adaptable. Consider these Scriptures:

Live in harmony with one another; do not be haughty (snobbish, high-minded, exclusive), but readily adjust yourself to [people, things] and give yourselves to humble tasks. Never overestimate yourself or be wise in your own conceits.

Repay no one evil for evil, but take thought for what is honest and proper and noble [aiming to be above reproach] in the sight of everyone.

If possible, as far as it depends on you live at peace with everyone.

Romans 12:16–18

Close examination of these verses quickly shows us that we cannot live in harmony with one another if our attitude is not right. We need a humble attitude, one that is willing to adapt and adjust to other people and situations. We should always stand up for what we believe is right, but in minor matters and ones where we can adapt to others, we should make an effort to do so.

It is not good for anyone to always get their own way. We need the experience of submitting to one another in humility and love. We all need to give in to others and prefer them and their desires at times. And we need to do it with a good attitude.

Most of our married life, Dave always let me choose where to eat when we were eating out. Being an easygoing person, it didn't matter to him that much. But it did and still does matter to me. Over the past few years, for some reason he has gotten very picky about where and what he eats, and suddenly he doesn't seem to want to eat where I do most of the time. He has decided that he doesn't like garlic, and Italian food is my favorite, so I'm sure you can see the problem brewing. I also like Chinese food, and although he is willing to eat it sometimes, it can't be greasy or have an aftertaste. I can see the writing on the wall, so to speak, and I know that I'm going to need to adapt. I've always been picky about where I eat, so I guess it's his turn to be picky if he wants to.

I will admit that this has been a little hard for me. Anytime we get our own way in something for a long time, it is difficult when suddenly things change. But I have reminded myself that Dave has let me choose where we eat for forty-four years, so it really is his turn. Sometimes we can manage to be adaptable more easily if we don't respond emotionally and take the time to reason with ourselves a little.

The Scripture above also tells us not to overestimate ourselves. We should never think that what we want is more important than what others want. We all have equal value and equal rights; keeping that in mind helps us adapt to the desires of others.

Increase Your Prayer Power

Prayer is the greatest privilege we have and one that opens the door to tremendous power and blessing in our lives and the lives of others. God hears and answers our prayers, but He tells us we must pray without anger and in agreement.

> I desire therefore that in every place men should pray, without anger or quarreling or resentment or doubt [in their minds], lifting up holy hands.
>
> *1 Timothy 2:8*

This Scripture states plainly that we are to pray without anger. In Mark chapter 11 we are told that when we pray, we must first forgive anyone that we have anything against. It is another verse that verifies that we cannot pray with a heart full of anger and strife and expect our prayers to get answers.

There are many, many angry people in the world today, and a large proportion of them are Christians who know better. They pray and mistakenly think that their anger doesn't matter. They may feel justified in their anger, but God condemns it and says we must let it go before praying. The best way to approach God in prayer is to first repent of all your own sins and then make sure you have no unforgiveness in your heart toward anyone else. How can we expect God to forgive us if we are refusing to forgive other people? I am sure that our offenses against God are much more serious than those of other people toward us.

A husband and wife or a family unit has tremendous power in prayer if they make a commitment to live in agreement.

> Again I tell you, if two of you on earth agree (harmonize together, make a symphony together) about whatever [anything and everything] they may ask, it will come to pass and be done for them by My Father in heaven.
>
> *Matthew 18:19*

This Scripture is truly amazing, and if any one of us really believes what it says, then we should certainly make a commitment to live in unity and harmony. Our foolish pride is not worth the price we pay in loss of power in prayer.

At one time in my life, I foolishly thought that I could argue with Dave anytime I felt like it and then when we needed a breakthrough in some area of our life, we could come together and pray what was commonly called "the prayer of agreement." But as we can see from Matthew 18:19, that type of prayer won't work. The kind of power God is talking about is only available to those who make a commitment to do their utmost to be makers and maintainers of peace. If anyone does that, God is so pleased that He will honor his or her prayers in a special way. It was right after this verse that Peter

asked Jesus how many times he had to forgive his
brother. Peter wanted this kind of power in prayer,
but it appears that he was recognizing that he had
a problem with one or some of the other disciples.
He was asking just how far Jesus expected him to
go in keeping peace. The answer that Jesus gave
was essentially that Peter needed to forgive however
many times it was necessary to stay in unity.

> Then Peter came up to Him and said, Lord,
> how many times may my brother sin against
> me and I forgive him and let it go? [As many
> as] up to seven times?
>
> *Matthew 18:21*

I am sure that Peter thought he was being very
generous, so Jesus' answer must have been shocking
for him.

> Jesus answered him, I tell you, not up to seven
> times, but seventy times seven!
>
> *Matthew 18:22*

That comes to four hundred and ninety times,
but even that is simply Jesus' way of saying, "Forgive as often as you must and don't put limits on it."
    Prayer is too precious a gift and too pow-
erful a privilege for us to mess it up by living in

disagreement. Take time before you pray to search your heart, and if you need to make things right with anyone you know, be the aggressor in bringing peace.

The Word of God even tells us that when we bring our gift to the altar, if we remember that our brother has aught against us, we should leave our gift and go make peace with our brother (Matt. 5:24). This is certainly teaching us to be the aggressor in peacemaking.

Power in Service

There is great power available to us as we give our lives to serving God. Jesus sent the disciples out two by two and told them to preach the Gospel and heal the sick. He also told them to find a house to stay in where they could dwell in peace (Luke 10:-1–9). He knew they couldn't have turmoil in their spirits and have His power flow through them at the same time. The promise He gave them was certainly worth any effort they had to make to remain in harmony.

Behold! I have given you authority and power to trample upon serpents and scorpions, and [physical and mental strength and ability]

over all the power that the enemy [possesses];
and nothing shall in any way harm you.

Luke 10:19

I want this promise to be a reality in my own
life and I am sure that you do, too. So let us make
the commitment to dwell in unity, harmony, and
agreement. That doesn't mean we should always
think like other people or even agree with their
choices, but it does mean that we agree not to fight
about it. A great deal of strife can be avoided by us
simply minding our own business. A good thing to
remember is that if we have no responsibility in a
matter, then we don't need to have an opinion.

Quite often we give our opinion when no one
has asked for it or wants it, and it becomes the
source of an argument or an offense. I am the type
of person who could be very free with my opinions,
but I've asked the Holy Spirit to help me use wisdom to keep them to myself unless they are asked
for. I have not yet arrived at the place of perfection
in this area, but I am continually learning how
important it is.

The apostle Paul wrote a letter to the Philippian
church in which he encouraged two women named
Euodia and Syntyche to get along. He even encouraged other people to help these two women get along
and keep cooperating as they toiled in spreading

the Gospel (Phil. 4:2–3). We don't know exactly what their strife was about, but perhaps part of their problem was excessive opinions about each other's choices. Paul must have heard that these two women were having difficulty getting along, and knowing that it would weaken the power of their ministry, he took time to write a letter in which he included special instruction to them in this matter. What Paul wrote to the two women is also written to us. If we want power in service for God, we must get along with each other. We must have unity!

The apostle Paul in writing to the Philippians said:

> Fill up and complete my joy by living in harmony and being of the same mind and one in purpose, having the same love, being in full accord and of one harmonious mind and intention.
>
> *Philippians 2:2*

All the truly great men and women we read about in the Bible were committed to unity. They knew that their service for God would be powerless without it. In the early days of our ministry, Dave and I received revelation from God concerning the dangers of strife. Strife is not just a little problem, but it is dangerous. If it is not stopped, it spreads like a contagious disease. I hate strife and what it does to people's lives, and I work diligently to keep it out of my life.

> Strive to live in peace with everybody and pursue that consecration and holiness without which no one will [ever] see the Lord.
> Exercise foresight and be on the watch to look [after one another], to see that no one falls back from and fails to secure God's grace (His unmerited favor and spiritual blessing), in order that no root of resentment (rancor, bitterness, or hatred) shoots forth and causes trouble and bitter torment, and the many become . . . defiled by it.
>
> *Hebrews 12:14–15*

This Scripture teaches us that we must strive (diligently work) to keep strife out of our lives. As I've said, that will require a lot of humility and willingness to be aggressive in being a peacemaker. It means we must give up our right to be right, mind our own business, and quite often we will need to refrain from saying something that we would like to say but is only going to cause trouble.

I have spent a good deal of time teaching on this subject as well as others that will promote unity among people. Life is miserable when we have no peace, and the truth is that when we have no peace, then we have no power.

We should help one another stay out of strife. We have a pastor on our staff who has many wonderful gifts, but one of the things he is especially good at is "conflict resolution." If we have a department or even two employees who have allowed strife to get into their relationship, he works with them and helps them find a resolution to their strife and disunity. We know that our service for the Lord will be weakened if we don't have unity.

Quite often we find that strife comes from a lack of proper communication. Many relationships are destroyed due to it, and it is sad because we can learn good communication skills if we really want to. Our pastor helps people in conflict communicate, and that almost always solves the problem. If it doesn't solve the problem and we find that one or more of the parties involved is determined to keep strife stirred up, then we know that Joyce Meyer Ministries is not the right place for them to work. We must have unity so we can be effective for God.

Two men we read about in the Bible, Abraham and Lot, had conflict between their herdsmen over grazing rights for their cattle. Abraham, being a very wise man, quickly went to Lot and said, "Let there be no strife between us." Then he offered Lot whatever portion of land he wanted and stated that he was willing to take what was left. We see Abraham humbling himself in this situation and shutting the door to future disunity. Lot chose the best portion of the land for himself, but God blessed Abraham even more than before because of his willingness to keep the peace (Gen. 13).

I have used this story as a reminder to help me keep strife out of my life, and I use it frequently in teaching. If you humble yourself and keep strife out of your life, God will bless you tremendously and you will have power in prayer and service, as well as the enjoyment of peace.

I want to close this chapter with a final reminder that the only way we can dwell in unity is if we are generous in mercy and forgiveness. God has given us a key to peace in teaching us to forgive those who harm us, and we can trust Him to bring justice and vindication in our lives anytime it is needed. Our part is to forgive and His part is to bring justice. You do your job, and let God do His.

Be eager and strive earnestly to guard and keep the harmony and oneness of [and produced by] the Spirit in the binding power of peace.

Ephesians 4:3

CHAPTER
13

Have Mercy upon Me, Oh God

Forgiving others their offenses is much easier when we are truly aware of our own sins and shortcomings. God never asks us to do for another what He has not first done for us. God shows us forgiveness before beginning to teach us of our need to forgive others. God wants to have relationship with us, He wants unity and harmony with us; therefore, He must forgive us.

Forgiveness is preceded by God's great grace and mercy. Mercy is actually one of the most beautiful attributes of God. Mercy is a great thing and something that we should marvel at. Here on earth we more or less expect it, but I think in heaven the angels are awed by God's mercy. The Christian writer and minister Andrew Murray said, "The omniscience of God is a wonder, the omnipotence of God is a wonder, God's spotless holiness is a wonder, but the greatest wonder of all is the mercy of God."

God completely forgives and restores to fellowship with Himself the most wretched of sinners. He is good to those who don't deserve it at all. If we would realize how many times in one day God forgives us for something we have thought, said, or done, we would not find it such a difficult chore to forgive others who have sinned against us. We should lift our voices to God many times each day and say, "Have mercy on me, oh God, and help me have mercy on others."

God never asks us to do anything without equipping us to do it. He never asks us to give to another what He has not first given to us. He gives us unconditional love and asks us to love others unconditionally. He gives us mercy and asks us to be merciful. He forgives us and asks us to forgive others. Is it too much to ask? I don't think it is.

The Bible teaches us that to whom much is given, much is required (Luke 12:48). God gives much and therefore has a right to expect a great deal from us. Take some time and recall your life and try to remember how much God has been willing to forgive you for. Have you been guilty of committing the same sin multiple times? Has God in His mercy worked with you and continually forgiven you until you learned to do right? Of course the answer is yes. It is yes for all of us.

What Has God Done for Us in Christ?

Through the sacrifice of Jesus Christ, God has drawn us to Himself out of darkness into the light. He finds us in our sin and misery and offers us a brand-new life. If we simply say "yes" to Him, He completely forgives all of our sins and puts us in right standing with Him by His grace and mercy. He not only forgives our sins, but He puts them as far as the East is from the West and He remembers them no more (Heb. 10:17; Ps. 103:12). He lifts us out of the pit of despair and makes our lives significant (James 4:10), and the amazing beauty is that we don't deserve any of it. We have done nothing worthy of the grace of God, nor can we ever do anything worthy of it. Forgiveness is definitely a gift. It is one we receive and one that we must be willing to give away. It is not only a gift that we give to others, but it is truly a gift that we give to ourselves. When we forgive another person, we give ourselves peace of mind, renewed energy, and time to do constructive things rather than fret and ruminate, just to name a few.

Mercy is kindness beyond what is reasonable. In other words, there is no reason for God's kindness that can be found. He is kind, and we are the blessed recipients of His kindness.

God in Christ has redeemed us, justified us, sanctified us, and is ever in the process of restoring us. Let us be ever thankful for the mercy of God. I need mercy today and every day. I am awed by God's great mercy, and my awe expands as I take the time to actually think about what God has done for me.

Are you struggling right now with the issue of forgiving someone who has wronged or hurt you? If you are, I would like to suggest that you take just fifteen minutes and seriously think about how much God has forgiven you for. I believe it will humble you, and then you will find it easy to forgive the ones who have wronged you.

Oh my friend, please forgive! Don't spend another day of your life bitter and angry over something that has happened and cannot now be undone. Don't live your life in reverse. Ask God to make you better, not bitter. Trust Him to work good things out of whatever unjust thing has happened to you. Remember, your part is to obey God and forgive, and His part is to restore and bring vindication. Don't waste one more precious day of your life with an unforgiving spirit. Ask God to work the same attitude in you that He has...a merciful and forgiving attitude.

Jesus is not harsh and hard. He is merciful, slow to anger, ready to forgive, and ready to help (Matt. 11:28–30). Jesus teaches us that He desires mercy and not sacrifice (Matt. 12:7). We can look at this Scripture from two viewpoints. First, we can see that God wants to give us mercy and that He is not interested in our sacrifices. Jesus is the one and only final sacrifice that will ever be needed. Our sacrifices are useless under the New Covenant. We can only turn to Jesus and ask for mercy when we sin, and He is ever ready to give it. I like the thought that God is ready to forgive. We don't have to wait for Him to get ready, we don't have to talk Him into it...He is ready to forgive. He has already made His decision to always be merciful and forgiving. We can do the same thing. We can set our mind ahead of time so that when offenses come our way, we are ready to forgive!

The second viewpoint we can have on this Scripture is that God wants us to give others mercy and not require sacrifices from them. It is man's glory to overlook an offense (Prov. 19:11). We have the privilege to overlook the things that others have done to hurt us. God has equipped us to do it. Offense will come to us, but we do not have to take it.

When someone hurts us, we can try to make

them pay by making them feel bad or continually harping on the matter; we can shut them out of our lives and refuse to talk to them. This is our human way of requiring sacrifices from others to pay for their sin against us. But we do have another option. We can be merciful.

What Does God Expect from Us?

God knows every sin we will commit before we commit it. He knows our frame, that we are but dust, and He does not expect us to never make mistakes. It was a great comfort to me when God spoke to my heart and said, "Joyce, you are no surprise to Me." God is never surprised by our trials, but He has our deliverance planned before the trouble even gets to us. God is never surprised by our mistakes and carnal ways. He has already decided to be merciful. What God does expect is for us to love Him and want His will. He wants us to be quick to repent and work with His Holy Spirit toward spiritual maturity. He is not angry if we have not arrived, but He does expect to find us pressing toward the mark of perfection.

The apostle Paul said that his one goal was to let go of what was behind and press toward the goal of perfection (Phil. 3:13). Just imagine that Paul, who received and wrote two-thirds of the New Testament, was still pressing on. I am so glad that God included this example in the Bible. It encourages me to know that God knows me thoroughly and realizes that I am a born- again human whose heart has been renewed but whose soul and body is still catching up with the great work He has done in my spirit.

The truth is that God doesn't expect us to never make mistakes. If we were able to live without sin, we would not need Jesus. But we do need Him every moment of every day. He is currently seated at the right hand of God interceding for us (Rom. 8:34). He continuously forgives our sins if we admit them and repent (1 John 1:9). God has definitely made provision for our faults, and it is by His great mercy that we can remain in fellowship and relationship with Him even though we are not yet perfected in all our behavior.

What Do You Expect from People?

We should expect to give mercy to others. They are not perfect and they will make mistakes. They will hurt and disappoint us, but the truth is that we do the same thing to them. We are usually unaware of what we do to hurt others, but we are very aware of what they do to hurt us.

I am not perfect, so why should I expect perfection from those I am in relationship with? I truly believe that our imperfections are why God has told us to be quick to forgive. He has made provision for all our mistakes by forgiving us and giving us the ability to forgive others if we are willing to do so. Dave and I have been married forty-four years as I write this book. We have forgiven each other thousands of times during those years, and we will need to forgive again and again as the rest of our years together go by.

We have learned to show one another mercy by often not even mentioning something the other one has done that irritates us. We can look over each other's faults and make allowances for them. I think that is a beautiful thought: "We can allow one another to make mistakes."

> Living as becomes you with complete lowliness of mind (humility) and meekness (unselfishness, gentleness, mildness), with patience, bearing with one another and making allowance, because you love one another.
>
> *Ephesians 4:2*

Years ago Dave and I stopped pressuring one another to be faultless. We realized how much God has to show us mercy, and we decided to do the same thing for each other. Making allowances for one another has helped us have a long-lasting, good marriage. Do a heart check. Do you pressure your spouse, family, or friends to be perfect, or to treat you perfectly? Are you harsh, hard, and demanding? Are you making allowances for people's weaknesses? Are you generous in mercy? These are good questions for all of us to ask ourselves occasionally. Answer them honestly, and if your attitude is not like Jesus', then ask Him to help you change it.

We must renew our mind and attitude daily. We don't always automatically have a good attitude. Sometimes we let things slide and have to renew our commitment to do things God's way. If you are at that point right now, it is nothing to be ashamed of. Rejoice that with God's help, you are seeing truth that will make you free.

What Did Jesus Expect of His Disciples?

Jesus purposely chose weak and foolish men to work with and through, so they could not take the glory that always belongs to God alone. Peter talked too much and was very prideful. He denied even knowing Jesus three times when the pressure was on, but Jesus showed him mercy and kindness. He forgave him, and Peter became a great apostle.

Thomas doubted a lot of what Jesus said, but He showed Thomas mercy and continued working with him. He even met Thomas in the midst of his doubt and unbelief and showed him His nail-scarred hands after His resurrection. Thomas had said that he would not believe unless he saw, and Jesus showed him what he needed to see instead of rejecting him for his doubting attitude.

The disciples at times displayed ridiculous behavior for a group of men who were traveling with Jesus. They argued over which of them was the greatest. They fell asleep when Jesus needed them and asked for them to pray with Him for one hour.

They were imperfect, but Jesus knew that when He chose them. He prayed all night before choosing the twelve men who would carry the Gospel to the then known world after His death and resurrection. Just imagine, twelve imperfect men who often lacked wisdom, doubted, showed pride, argued among themselves, and wanted to know how many times they had to forgive each other. Sounds a lot like us to me.

Learning to Receive Mercy

Like me, I am sure you know that you are very imperfect and that you need a lot of mercy. God is ready to give mercy, but do you know how to receive it? We may ask God to forgive us for our sins, but do we receive His forgiveness by forgiving ourselves? Are you holding a lot of past sins against yourself? I did that for years, and because of it, I was unable to show mercy to others. As I say frequently, "We cannot give away what we don't have."

Have you received mercy? As you read this book, are there things that you still feel guilty about even though you have sincerely repented? Have you taken time to ask God for mercy, and equally important, have you taken time to receive mercy from God? Mercy is a gift, but a gift has no value to us unless we receive it. Jesus said, "Ask, and... receive, that your joy may be full" (John 16:24 NKJV). Are you doing a lot of asking but very little receiving? If so, it is time for change. God has done everything that needs to be done for us in Christ. Now it is up to us to receive it by faith. Not by merit, but only by faith.

As we learn to receive God's outrageous mercy, we will be able to give it to others.

The Characteristics of a Merciful Attitude

Mercy Understands

Jesus is a merciful High Priest Who understands our weaknesses and infirmities because He has been tempted in every way that we are, yet He never sinned (Heb. 4:15). I love the fact that Jesus understands me. Since we each have our own weaknesses, we should also be able to understand when other people make mistakes and need mercy and forgiveness. Having an understanding heart is one of the beautiful characteristics of mercy. The next time someone mistreats you, try to be understanding. Perhaps this person feels ill or has had a bad day at work. Wrongful behavior certainly isn't right, but remember that gentle words turn away wrath. Kindness has the power to divert anger because good always overcomes evil (Rom. 12:21).

Dave was very understanding with me during the years I was recovering from the effects of sexual abuse in my childhood. Had he not shown me mercy, we probably would not be married today and both of us may well have missed God's great plan for our lives. Is there someone in your life right now whom you can try a little harder to understand? Ask them to tell you their story. Usually when people behave in dysfunctional ways, it is because something in their life has hurt them and they have never recovered.

The more we know about the background of people, the easier it is to understand any behavior they display that might be less than desirable.

Mercy Does Not Expose People's Faults
A person who is not controlled by the Holy Spirit usually has a morbid fondness for spreading bad news and especially telling the wrong things that others have done. God's Word states that love covers a multitude of sins (1 Pet. 4:8).

> Hatred stirs up contentions, but love covers all transgressions.
>
> *Proverbs 10:12*

Each proverb in the Bible is a point of wisdom that will make our lives better if we heed it. This proverb confirms what Peter said in the New Testament about covering sins instead of exposing them.

When Joseph finally had the opportunity to deal with his brothers regarding their cruel treatment of him, he did it privately (Gen. 45:1). He asked everyone else to leave the room when his brothers arrived because he didn't want anyone to know what they had done to him. He was not only ready to forgive them completely, but he kept their sin a secret so other people could like and respect them. He didn't want them to be embarrassed. These amazing character traits that Joseph had help reveal to us why God was able to use him so powerfully.

If we truly want to be used by God, we must have a merciful attitude.

When we have something against someone who has offended us, we should go to that person privately to discuss it (Matt. 18:15). If they refuse to listen, then we are told to take others with us to talk to them in the hopes of seeing them restored to a proper tone of mind and heart.

Do unto other people as you would have them do unto you. If you did something wrong, would you want people to spread the news of it around or keep it to themselves? I already know the answer because I know what I would want. I would want my sins covered and I am sure that you do, too.

Mercy Doesn't Judge

It is easy to judge and have critical opinions about people who make mistakes, but it is not wise. We are called by God to help people, not to judge them. As I mentioned earlier in this book, we may judge sin as being what it is, but we shouldn't judge individuals, because we don't know their heart or what they may have been through in their lives.

Mercy is greater than judgment!

For to him who has shown no mercy the judgment [will be] merciless, but mercy [full of glad confidence] exults victoriously over judgment.

James 2:13

It is human to judge, but it is godly to give mercy. Ask God to help you develop a merciful attitude and look for the characteristic traits of mercy in your life. To judge means to set oneself up as God. Only God has the right to judge people because He is the only One Who knows all the facts. I don't want to be guilty of trying to be God in another person's life, so I try really hard to avoid judging others. Certainly, I wasn't always like that. I was very judgmental for a long time, but the good news is that we can all change with God's help.

Mercy Believes the Best

Love always believes the best of every person, and mercy is a trait of love. Mercy doesn't pass sentence without a fair trial. Mercy wants to know the truth, not just mere hearsay. I hate it when people tell me something bad about someone else, especially if it is merely gossip and not a proven fact. I have to work harder to believe the best after hearing the worst. We should always believe the best until a charge against someone has been proven.

I know that I have been publicly accused of

things I did not do, and I really appreciated the people who said, "I don't believe that Joyce would do that." I did not appreciate the people who took what they heard, added to it, and passed ugly rumors to other people.

We are so much happier if we believe the best instead of being suspicious and quick to believe every evil thing we hear about another person.

Mercy Is for Everyone

I have noticed that it is easier for me to show mercy to people I love and have a good relationship with. It is more difficult when I don't particularly care for the one I need to be merciful to. However, true mercy is merciful to everyone. A merciful attitude is not something we turn on and off; it is part of our character... it is who we are. We never say "I do mercy," but we do say "I am merciful."

Equality is important to God. He is no respecter of persons, and He doesn't want us to be, either. All people are equally important to God. They are all His children, and He extends mercy to all. As His representatives in the earth, we should strive to do the same thing. Don't behave by how you "feel" toward a person, but be merciful and it will enrich your own life.

In the Bible we see a story commonly referred to as the story of the Good Samaritan. It is about a man who stopped to help another man who was injured and lying on the side of road. It was not anyone that he knew, but he used his time and money to help a stranger (Luke 10:27–37). Truly, the merciful man shows mercy to everyone—not just those he knows, likes, and wants to impress. This "good Samaritan" was a great man in the eyes of God simply because he noticed, stopped, and showed mercy to a man he had never seen before that day and probably would never see again. It cost the Good Samaritan time and money to help the injured man; he gained nothing material from his actions, but he still did the right thing. Anytime we do the right thing, it gives us inner peace and we reap a reward in due time. Try to help more people. Show them the mercy and the undeserved kindness of God. I am sure we would all agree that the world needs more "good Samaritans," so let it begin with us.

CHAPTER
14

Lighten Your Load

I recently watched a movie in which a man was carrying a secret that, if he told it, would release another man from jail where he was serving a life sentence for a crime he did not commit. However, if he told the secret, it might well get him into a great deal of trouble because there were warrants out for his arrest. He asked why he should come forward and put himself in danger in order to set another man free who meant nothing to him. The lawyer who was prompting him to be truthful said, "Because if you tell the truth, you can unburden yourself, and it will be one less heavy load you will have to carry through life." He was basically saying, "Do yourself a favor and do the right thing."

We continually make choices in life about how we will respond to circumstances in our lives. God pleads with us in His Word to make the right choices, but He still leaves the choice to us. Whether or not we forgive those whom we would class as our "enemies" is one of those choices we frequently face in life. If we make the right choice, we lighten our load, but if we make the wrong one, we actually burden and torment ourselves.

> Then his master called him and said to him, You contemptible and wicked attendant! I forgave and cancelled all that [great] debt of yours because you begged me to.
>
> And should you not have had pity and mercy on your fellow attendant, as I had pity and mercy on you?
>
> And in wrath his master turned him over to the torturers (the jailers), till he should pay all that he owed.
>
> So also My heavenly Father will deal with every one of you if you do not freely forgive your brother from your heart his offenses.
>
> *Matthew 18:32–35*

This chapter in the Bible is one where Peter asked Jesus how many times he had to forgive his brother when he sinned against him. Jesus told Peter a story about a man who owed the king an amount of money that would total ten thousand dollars today. The king wanted to settle the account, but the man could not pay and asked for mercy. The king's heart was moved with compassion, and he forgave (cancelled) the debt. The same man who had just been forgiven went and found someone who owed him about twenty dollars, and he put his hands around his throat and demanded that he be paid.

This debtor fell down and began begging for mercy, but instead of forgiving him as he had been forgiven, the man whom the king had forgiven put the debtor in prison. When his master saw his behavior, he reminded him of the mercy he had received and told him that he would be tortured because of his unwillingness to forgive.

This story that Jesus told deserves our diligent study. It sums up all that I am trying to say in this book. God forgives us for more than anyone could ever possibly owe us, and we must learn to be as merciful and forgiving as He is. We should never try to make anyone "pay" for what they have done to hurt us. Jesus paid our debts and freely forgives us, and He expects us to do the same thing for others. If we don't, then we will be tortured in our souls just as Jesus said in Matthew chapter 18. We can lighten our load by doing the right thing and forgiving.

Ralph Waldo Emerson said, "For every minute you are angry you lose sixty seconds of happiness." It is a fact that we forfeit our joy to hang on to our anger, and I can tell you from experience in my own life that it is not worth it. Marcus Aurelius said, "How much more grievous are the consequences of anger than the causes of it." We may initially feel angered over a rather minor incident, but if we feed that spark of anger with negative thoughts about the individual who angered us, the consequences of the anger will definitely seem more grievous than what initially caused it. Perhaps we should live by the Chinese proverb that says, "If you are patient in one moment of anger, you will escape a hundred days of sorrow."

Throughout the centuries great men and women have experienced the torment of unforgiveness and the joy of forgiveness. Here are a few of the things they have said:

> "There was never an angry man that thought his anger unjust."—St. Francis de Sales
> "Consider how much more you often suffer from your anger and grief, than from those very things for which you are angry and grieved."—Marcus Antonius
> "Anger, if not restrained, is frequently more hurtful to us than the injury that provokes it."—Seneca

"Whatever is begun in anger, ends in shame."
—Benjamin Franklin

"People who fly into a rage always make a bad landing."—Will Rogers

"Forgiveness does not change the past, but it does enlarge the future."—Paul Boese

"Marriage is three parts love and seven parts forgiveness."—Lao Tzu

"To forgive is the highest, most beautiful form of love. In return, you will receive untold peace and happiness."—Robert Mueller

"You will know that forgiveness has begun when you recall those who hurt you and feel the power to wish them well."—Lewis B. Smedes

Anger Is on the Rise

The statistics on anger are a strong reminder that there is a lot of it around. Almost a third of people who were polled on the subject (32%) say they have a close friend or family member who has trouble controlling their anger. One in five (20%) say they have ended a relationship or friendship with someone because of how that person behaved when they were angry. If you are an angry person, it would be wise to realize that the people you love may not always be willing to hang around and put up with your temper. Sadly, we frequently take our bad moods out on the people we love the most. I suppose we do this because we erroneously think they will just continue forgiving and understanding us, but that may not last forever. Everyone has their limits, and when pushed beyond them, the damage is often irreparable.

Some of the things people are angry about today are really ridiculous. People get so angry at their cell phones when they are not working properly that they may throw them across the room or into a pond of water. I can remember when we had to find a pay phone on the side of the road if we wanted to make a call while driving. We had to park, get out of the car, and have the exact change. If the weather was hot or cold, we had to suffer the discomfort. We didn't think anything about it, because it was just what one did if they wanted to make a call while traveling. Now we get angry if we are driving and pass through an area where there is no cell tower and we have to wait two minutes to get to one before making our call.

We now have "road rage," "web rage," and "office rage." What Jesus called ungodly behavior, we now call an emotional disease that requires counseling. Are we merely making excuses for a lack of self-control? Have we become so utterly selfish that we really think everything in life should be exactly the way we want it to be all the time?

Many people are angry because they are unhappy, and they are unhappy because they are angry. It becomes a vicious cycle of more and more anger, and I truly believe the only answer is a right (biblical) mind-set and a willingness to forgive the things and people in life who displease us.

According to the *Sunday Times Magazine* for July 16, 2006, 45 percent of people regularly lose their temper at work. They are angry with people! People they work with, people they work for, and people who make the rules at work. If you are an angry person, it is not difficult to find something or someone to be angry with.

About 64 percent of Britons working in an office have had office rage. These problems seem to exist much more or perhaps even exclusively in affluent countries. I have been to the poorest parts of India and Africa several times each. A person in India who is blessed enough to have a job often works for less than a dollar a day. A woman may work quietly day after day in the hot sun sweeping the street for shopkeepers, and she definitely doesn't have "street sweepers' rage." It seems to me that the more we have, the angrier we become. Forty years ago I didn't have any temptation to get angry at my cell phone or computer because I didn't have one. Life wasn't as stressful and people were not as angry in those days. Have we really made progress? I guess in some ways we have, but in others ways we have digressed miserably.

Of current Internet users, 71 percent admit to having suffered net rage, and 50 percent of us have reacted to computer problems by hitting our PC, hurling parts of it around, screaming or abusing our colleagues. If it weren't so sad, it would make a hilarious comedy. At least 33 percent of Britons are not on speaking terms with their neighbors, and I am sure the percentage is no less in America and other so-called civilized parts of the world.

More than 80 percent of drivers say they have been involved in road rage incidents; 25 percent have committed an act of road rage. One dare not make a mistake while driving, like failing to give a signal when changing lanes or accidentally cutting someone off in another lane. Someone is likely to display rage that they have experienced inconvenience because of an imperfect driver.

The world is what it is, and the way things are going, it is not likely to change for the better, but we are not left without an answer to the problems we face. Even if the world doesn't change, we can change. Each one of us can take responsibility for how we respond to outward stimuli, and we can choose to live a life of peace and harmony. We may have to forgive a hundred times each day, but it is still better than seething inside with anger or expressing our anger in ways that end up embarrassing us.

Don't Go There

> Enter through the narrow gate; for wide is the gate and spacious and broad is the way that leads away to destruction, and many are those who are entering through it. But the gate is narrow (contracted by pressure) and the way is straitened and compressed that leads away to life, and few are those who find it.
>
> *Matthew 7:13–14*

We can see from this Scripture that there are two roads we can take in life. One of the roads is broad and easy to walk on. It has plenty of room for all our emotions, and we will never get lonely because this is the road that most people walk on. On this wide road, we have room for all of our anger, bitterness, resentment, and unforgiveness, but the road leads to destruction. Go ahead, read the Scripture again... yes, it leads to destruction. There is another road we can choose... it is the road that Jesus traveled.

History is dotted with men and women who

have chosen the narrow road also, and they are usually the ones we remember and want to model our lives after. I don't know about you, but I have never wanted to be like Hitler or the Boston Strangler. They were angry men who were so tormented that they became obsessed with tormenting others. We can easily see that their lives ended in destruction because they took the wrong path. No, I have never yearned to be like them, but I have wanted to be like Ruth, Esther, Joseph, or Paul. I have read and reread the story of Joseph dozens of times over the years and studied the forgiving attitude Joseph displayed. I know that God blessed Joseph mightily in his lifetime and blessed his descendants because he took the narrow road.

Every blessing we enjoy today was bought with someone's sacrifice and pain. I believe my children and grandchildren and great-grandchildren will have better lives because I received God's grace to forgive my father for sexually abusing me. I could have taken the broad path. It was there staring me in the face, screaming, "Travel on me, you deserve an easy path after what you have been through." But that path is deceptive. It appears initially to be the easier path, but in the end it only adds misery to misery.

In the closing chapter of this book I will tell you the full story of how God led and taught me to forgive my father, but for now let's just say that I took the narrow road that leads to life. It was often a lonely road, not well traveled, but when I thought I couldn't go another mile, I would see Jesus up ahead saying, "Follow Me, I am leading you to a peaceful place."

When I am tempted to stay angry and bitter in my life now, I say to myself (often out loud), "Joyce, don't go there." We can feel ourselves descending into the dark waters of bitterness. If we go deep enough, we can feel the murky water closing over our heads and pressing us down, down, and down. Depression, self-pity, and a host of other negative emotions become our companions.

There Is a Place Called "There"

There is a place called "There," and we have all been there. Perhaps some of you are living "There" right now. It is a huge place, but somehow your life seems to be very small and confined. There is a huge mountain in "There," and it takes up most of the space. You spend a lot of your time going around and around the mountain and never making any real progress on your journey. All you need to do to live "There" is follow your emotions. Get angry when things don't go your way, or when people treat you unfairly, don't forgive them. Don't be merciful, and you can have a prime plot of land in "There."

The Israelites lived "There" for forty years. They called it The Wilderness, but I call it "There." "There" is anywhere we have been many times before that makes us miserable and steals the quality of life Jesus wants us to have. It may be self-pity, selfishness, greed, anger, resentment, hatred, revenge, or jealousy. The names that are given to "There" are endless, but the results of living "There" are all the same. Misery, torment, frustration, and emptiness are what fill the atmosphere in this broad place that leads to destruction.

As I said, I lived "There" a long, long time before I decided to get out of "There" and stay out of "There." When my emotions try to suck me back in, I have to resist them by calling on the grace and power of God. But I honestly cannot waste another day of my life "There."

"They" Are to Blame!

The Israelites blamed their enemies. It was always some enemy's fault that they were unhappy and miserable. The only real enemy they had was their bad attitude. They were unbelieving, complaining, greedy, jealous, unthankful, fearful, self-pitying, angry, and impatient. It is comforting to us to blame someone else for all of our problems. As long as "They" are the problem, we never have to look at ourselves and take responsibility for our actions.

For years I focused on what my father had done to me instead of my reaction to what he had done. God offered me an answer, but His way meant that I had to move out of "There" and stop thinking "They" were my problem. It was true that my father had hurt me terribly, but God was offering me healing and restoration...the choice was mine! Are you at the same crossroads in your life right now? If so, I implore you to get off the broad path that leads to destruction and step onto the narrow path that leads to life.

Who are "They" that are to blame for all of our problems? If you listen to yourself and others talk, it seems "They" have messed up our lives, and "They" need to fix it. "They" did, and "They" say, and we are afraid "They" will or won't do this or that. But who are "They"? Oh, "They" can be anyone, anytime in any place. The truth is that "They" have no power to ultimately harm us if we stay on the right path and follow Jesus. He is The Way to joy unspeakable, peace that passes understanding, and a life so amazing that we have no words to explain it. When I think of all the years

I lived "There," blaming "They" for all my misery, it makes me want to write book after book about what God offers us through Jesus Christ. I want you to know the truth because it will make you free. The truth is: You don't have to be angry and filled with bitterness and resentment when someone hurts you. You have another choice . . . YOU CAN FORGIVE!! The next time your emotions flare and you are invited to a land called Unforgiveness, be determined that you won't go "There."

No matter what happens in your life, keep a good attitude. Paul said that he had learned how to be content whether he was abased or abounding (Phil. 4:11). I am fully convinced that Paul learned the same way we do. He experienced the misery of making the wrong choices until he finally saw the wisdom of making the right ones. When he did, it brought him contentment.

Life Offers Offense

The people and circumstances in our life will offer us an opportunity to be offended, but we don't have to go "There." How will you respond? Will you blame "They" or will you take responsibility for your attitudes? We are told in God's Word to guard our heart with all vigilance (Prov. 4:23). It is our responsibility to work with the Holy Spirit to keep our heart free from offense toward God and man. Champions turn away from offense just as King David did many times in his life.

Are you ready to stand before God and have answer the question why you wasted your life living "There"? Do you really think that you can say "They" made me do it and have Him accept that answer? I think we all know better than that. It is time for each of us to take action in our own life and make a decision that we will not live angry and bitter.

The road is wide that leads to "There"; it seems a very small place even though the road to get there is wide and well traveled. It has a huge mountain in it and the only thing to do "There" is be miserable!

If you have ever been "There," or if you are "There" right now, then you know how miserable it makes you, so move out of "There." And as you go, say, "I won't be back!"

CHAPTER
15

God's Reward

According to the Bible, we cannot please God without faith, and those who come to Him must believe that He is, and that He is a rewarder of those who diligently seek Him (Heb. 11:6).

God is a rewarder! I love the thought of it, don't you? We all like rewards for our hard work, and I admit that living a forgiving lifestyle is hard work. It is not something we do right a few times and then move beyond it. It is something that we deal with throughout our lives and usually more frequently than we would like to. When I am doing something that is hard, it always helps me to remember that reward is on the other side of the pain.

A person works out at the gym three times a week even though it is hard work and often makes them sore because they look forward to the reward of better health and a muscular body instead of a flabby one.

We go to work for the reward of a much needed paycheck. We go to the grocery store for the reward of eating at home. I doubt that we would do much in life if there were no promise of reward. God says that every man will receive his reward for the things he has done in this life, whether they were good or bad (Rev. 22:12). He called Abraham to leave his family and home and go to a place that God would afterward show him. God promised Abraham that there would be a reward for his obedience (Gen. 12:1-2, 15:1).

When a child passes all the tests of each grade in school, his reward is that he graduates. We also must pass tests in this life. The forgiveness test is just one of them, but it is an important one, and when we pass it, we do receive God's reward. The reward may manifest in many ways. It comes in the form of peace and joy, but it can also come in the form of some kind of promotion in life. Joseph had to pass the forgiveness test before he was promoted to a position of power and authority in Egypt. Are you looking for promotion in life, but you're angry? If you are, then you will miss your reward.

We all have our own story, but since I am writing this book, I will tell you mine and I pray that it helps you.

*   *   *

I was born June 3, 1943. The day I was born my father was shipped overseas to be a soldier in World War II. I am told that I didn't see him again until I was three years old. I remember always being afraid of my father. It seems he was always shouting and angry about one thing or another. Of course, my mother and I always assumed it was something we had done, but then it also seemed that no matter what we did, he still found reason to be angry. For the first nine years of my life, it was just my mother and me in the house with dear old dad, but then my brother came along.

By then my father was already molesting me regularly, and I remember hoping with all my heart that when my mother gave birth, the baby would be another girl. In my childish foolishness, I thought if the baby was a girl that maybe my father would like her better than me and stop doing the things he did that made me feel bad and dirty.

The baby was a boy, not a girl, and I think I resented him for that for a while. Then we bonded, and I often felt that my brother, who was named

David, was my only friend in the family. He didn't know what my father was doing to me, but he had battles of his own to fight. He experienced the brunt of my father's anger also and started drinking and doing drugs at a very early age. When he was seventeen, he enlisted in the Marine Corps, went to fight in the Vietnam War, and was never the same again. (Actually, I am sad to say that while I was writing this book, my brother was found dead in a homeless shelter in California at the age of fifty-seven.)

I am sure someone is thinking right now, "Why is Joyce in ministry helping people all over the world, and her own brother was living in a homeless shelter?" My brother was in a homeless shelter because he refused to walk the narrow road that leads the way to life. We helped David at various intervals of his life, including having him live with us for a few years, but the end result was always the same. He once said to me, "Sis, I am not mean, I am just stupid."

He knew that he made bad choices, but for some reason I don't fully understand, he continued to make them. I think my brother's and my life are an interesting parallel. By God's grace I took the narrow road, and my life now is filled with God's reward. I am happy, content, blessed, and I have the privilege of helping people come to know the love and forgiveness of God and His reward in their own life. My brother took the wide road that led to destruction, and he is dead at age fifty-seven without ever having experienced God's reward fully. I think I can truly say that he wasted his life and nobody could get him to stop. He had a few good years while he lived with us, but as soon as he got out on his own, he went back to bad choices and bad results.

We were both hurt as children, and God offered both of us help and restoration, but we ended up at entirely different places in life due to our own choices. God loved us both and still does, but I know He is sad that my brother David missed so much. I know I am sad because of it, but it makes me even more determined than ever to keep sharing the truth with people. We overcome evil with good (Rom. 12:21) and my response to my brother's death can only be, "I will press in even more than before to help as many people as I can." If you have had disappointments in life that are trying to pull you down into apathy and inactivity, resist and be determined to come out of your heartache even stronger than before. Don't let your disappointments make you bitter, but instead, let them make you better.

My father sexually abused me for as long as I can

remember until I left home at the age of eighteen. I conservatively counted that he raped me at least two hundred times in my life between the ages of thirteen and eighteen. Prior to that he molested me. My father didn't force me physically, but he forced me with fear and intimidation, and the effect was brutal.

I went to my mother for help, but she didn't really know how to deal with what I was telling her, so she chose to not believe me and do nothing. She has since apologized, but it took her thirty years to do so, and by then I had already recovered through God's help. So I had a father who abused me and a mother who abandoned me, and then found myself with a God Who showed me I had to completely forgive them both. You might want to pause and think about that a little before you rush on to hear the rest of my story.

God Requires Obedience, Not Sacrifice

I prayed the "I forgive my enemies" prayer, and to some degree I did forgive them. God taught me that "hurting people hurt people." I realized that my father was a miserable man who had more than likely been hurt and that he was filled with a spirit of lust from incest in his own family bloodline.

I did a lot of talking to myself, and a lot of praying, and was able to stop hating my father, but I didn't realize until many years later that I still had a long way to go. I had given God a sacrifice, but He wanted complete obedience.

Once I was old enough to move away from home, I spent as little time with my parents as I absolutely had to. As they got older and their health began to fail, I sent some money their way occasionally and visited briefly on holidays. They had moved from St. Louis back to southeast Missouri where they were originally from, and I was thrilled. With them living two hundred miles away, I had even more of an excuse not to be around them much.

In the meantime, our ministry was growing and we were excited about helping people. God had led us to go on television, and I knew that I needed to have some kind of confrontation and conversation with my parents to let them know that I would be sharing my story on television in order to help other people. I didn't know how it would go, but I didn't really expect it to go well. I was pleasantly surprised when my father told me to do whatever I needed to do. He mentioned that he had no idea how his abuse would hurt me, but he still did not apologize or seem to have any desire to repent and seek a relationship with God.

A few more years went by; the ministry was

growing and things between my parents and me were about the same. They were getting older and their health was even worse, and since they didn't have enough money to live properly, we were sending them money on a regular basis. I felt it was quite noble of me to do even that and was shocked when God let me know that He expected me to do much more.

The True Meaning of Blessing Your Enemies

But love your enemies and be kind and do good [doing favors so that someone derives benefit from them] and lend, expecting and hoping for nothing in return but considering nothing as lost and despairing of no one; and then your recompense (your reward) will be great (rich, strong, intense, and abundant), and you will be sons of the Most High, for He is kind and charitable and good to the ungrateful and the selfish and wicked.

Luke 6:35

If you rushed past the reading of the Scripture above like we often do, please go back and really look at what it is saying. When does our reward come? It comes after we do good things for our enemies with a good attitude.

One morning I was praying, and I felt God whisper in my heart that He wanted us to bring my parents back to St. Louis, buy them a house close to us, and take care of them until they died. I immediately assumed the idea was just the devil trying to torment me, and I strongly resisted it and tried to forget it. However, when God is trying to talk to us, He will be rather repetitive until we finally listen. The idea kept coming back to me, especially when I was trying to pray. Imagine God trying to talk to me when I was praying! I am sure I was busy telling Him everything I wanted and needed, and He was trying to interrupt me long enough to tell me what He wanted.

I finally thought I would present the idea to Dave, who I was hoping would tell me that it was ridiculous and that would be the end of it. That was one time I was fully prepared to submit to my husband! I wanted him to tell me no, but he didn't. He simply said, "If that is what you think God is leading you to do, then we'd better obey Him."

Dave and I didn't have much money saved, and it would take most of what we had, if not all of it, to do what God was asking. My parents not only needed a house but a car and furniture as well, because nothing they had was very nice. God had made it clear to me that He wanted us to take "good" care of them and treat them as if they had been the best parents in the world.

My flesh was screaming all the way! How could God ask me to do this? Had He forgotten that they had never done anything for me? Didn't God care that they had hurt me terribly and never been there for me in any way when I needed them? Didn't God know or care how I felt?

Without any positive emotions to spur me on, I did everything God asked me to do. My parents moved back to St. Louis, they lived eight minutes from our house, and we took care of their every need. The older they got, the more needs they had. My father showed some verbal appreciation, but he still remained the same mean and cranky man he had always been.

Three years had gone by since we took over their care, and on Thanksgiving morning my mother called and said that my dad had been crying all week and wanted to know if I could come over and talk to him about something. Dave and I went, and my dad asked me to forgive him for what he had done to me when I was a child. He cried and cried, and he also asked Dave to forgive him. He said,

"Most men would have hated me, but Dave, you never did anything but love me." We assured him that we forgave him and asked him if he wanted to ask God to forgive him and receive Jesus Christ as his Savior. He assured us that he did, and so we prayed and my father was born again right there on the spot. He asked if I would baptize him, and ten days later we did at our church in the inner city of St. Louis. I can truly say that for the next four years, I saw a true change in my father. He died at the age of eighty-six, and I know he is in heaven.

When God talked to me about buying them a house, I didn't realize the fruit I would eventually see. The love that God's grace showed my father through us melted his hard heart and opened the way for him to see the light. My mother is still alive as of this writing. She is eighty-seven and lives in an assisted living facility that we pay for. She is a child of God, and although her health is not great, she seems to enjoy each day of her life. I was saddened that she had to endure hearing about my brother's death, but God gave her a lot of grace and she is doing quite well with the news.

The Scripture that I quoted above says we are to do favors for our enemies and be kind to them... *then* our reward will be great! I had spent years giving God a sacrifice but not true obedience. I did what I absolutely had to do for my parents, and even that I did a bit resentfully, but God had more in mind. He had more in His mind for me to do, and more for me to receive. I received a greater release in my own soul, knowing that I had fully obeyed God. I received the joy of leading my father, who had raped me over two hundred times, to the Lord and then baptizing him. We also firmly believe that God opened the door for us to help millions more people after we had fully obeyed Him. We began translating our television program into foreign languages, and it now airs in two-thirds of the world in more than forty different languages. Multiplied thousands are receiving Jesus as their Savior and learning the Word of God through that outreach.

God is truly amazing! He gives us the grace to do things that in ourselves, we would not, and never could, do. How could I love the man who had been the source of my torment? How could I love the mother who abandoned me in the situation and didn't help me when I asked her to? Because God has a plan that is very different from ours, He enables us to do things we cannot imagine that we would ever do, including forgiving those who have misused and abused us. God is good, and if we will let Him, He wants to let His goodness flow through us to others.

You have heard the fast-forward version of my

story. I know that most of you have a story of your own, and perhaps your story is even more shocking than mine. God wants to give you double blessing for your former trouble. He wants you to live in the midst of His abundant reward. Don't let anything stop you. Do yourself a favor...FORGIVE!!

ABOUT THE AUTHOR

JOYCE MEYER is one of the world's leading practical Bible teachers. A #1 *New York Times* bestselling author, she has written more than ninety inspirational books, including *Living Beyond Your Feelings, Power Thoughts,* the entire Battlefield of the Mind family of books, and two novels, *The Penny* and *Any Minute,* as well as many others. She has also released thousands of audio teachings, as well as a complete video library. Joyce's *Enjoying Everyday Life*® radio and television programs are broadcast around the world, and she travels extensively conducting conferences. Joyce and her husband, Dave, are the parents of four grown children and make their home in St. Louis, Missouri.

JOYCE MEYER MINISTRIES
U.S. & FOREIGN OFFICE ADDRESSES

Joyce Meyer Ministries
P.O. Box 655
Fenton, MO 63026
USA
(636) 349-0303
www.joycemeyer.org

Joyce Meyer Ministries—Canada
P.O. Box 7700
Vancouver, BC V6B 4E2
Canada
(800) 868-1002

Joyce Meyer Ministries—Australia
Locked Bag 77
Mansfield Delivery Centre
Queensland 4122
Australia
(07) 3349 1200

Joyce Meyer Ministries—England
P.O. Box 1549
Windsor SL4 1GT
United Kingdom
01753 831102

Joyce Meyer Ministries—South Africa
P.O. Box 5
Cape Town 8000
South Africa
(27) 21-701-1056

OTHER BOOKS BY JOYCE

*Battlefield of the Mind** (over three million copies sold)
*Power Thoughts**
*Living Beyond Your Feelings**
*Eat the Cookie…Buy the Shoes**
Never Give Up!
I Dare You
The Penny
The Power of Simple Prayer
*The Confident Woman**
Look Great, Feel Great
*Approval Addiction**
*The Love Revolution**
Any Minute
Start Your New Life Today
21 Ways to Finding Peace and Happiness
A New Way of Living
Woman to Woman
100 Ways to Simplify Your Life
The Secret to True Happiness
Reduce Me to Love
The Secret Power of Speaking God's Word

DEVOTIONALS

Love Out Loud Devotional
The Confident Woman Devotional
Hearing from God Each Morning
New Day, New You Devotional
Battlefield of the Mind Devotional
*Ending Your Day Right**
*Starting Your Day Right**

*Also available in Spanish